Caring for Folks from Birth to Death

Caring for Folks from Birth to Death

James E. Hightower, Jr.
Editor/Contributor

BROADMAN PRESS
Nashville, Tennessee

© Copyright 1985 • Broadman Press

4224-15
ISBN: 0-8054-2415-6

Dewey Decimal Classification: 253.5
Subject Headings: PASTORAL WORK//COUNSELING
Library of Congress Catalog Card Number: 84-20005
Printed in the United States of America

Unless otherwise indicated Scripture quotations are from the King James Version of the Bible.

Verses marked (GNB) are from the *Good News Bible*,the Bible in Today's English Version. Old Testament: Copyright © American Bible Society 1976: New Testament: Copyright © American Bible Society 1966, 1971, 1976. Used by permission.

Verses marked NASB are from the *New American Standard Bible.* Copyright © The Lockman Foundation, 1960, 1962, 1963, 1971, 1972, 1973, 1975. Used by permission.

Verses marked (NEB) are from *The New English Bible,* © Delegates of Oxford University Press and the Syndics of the Cambridge University Press, 1961, 1970. Reprinted by permission.

Verses marked (NIV) are from the HOLY BIBLE *New International Version,* copyright © 1978, New York Bible Society. Used by permission.

Verses marked RSV are from the Revised Standard Version of the Bible, copyrighted 1946, 1952, © 1971, 1973 by the National Council of the Churches of Christ in the U.S.A., and used by permission.

Library of Congress Cataloging in Publication Data
Main entry under title:

Caring for folks from birth to death.

Bibliography: p.
1. Pastoral psychology—Addresses, essays,
lectures. I. Hightower, James E.
BV4012.C319   1985   253   84-20005
ISBN 0-8054-2415-6 (pbk.)

Preface

As I have traveled around the United States leading pastoral care workshops, I sensed a gap in the pastoral care literature. Ministers need a concise handbook that will help them quickly grasp the developmental issues that persons face and give them some ideas of how the church can effectively minister to these folks.

I began reading the literature from Lewis Sherrill (*The Struggle of the Soul*) to Gail Sheehy (*Passages* and *Pathfinders*) to Daniel Levinson (*The Seasons of a Man's Life*) to Roger Gould (*Transformations*). Nowhere were the two issues of development and ministry coupled in the fashion that I envisioned. Knowing I could not handle that large task by myself, I contacted six of the most competent theorists and practictioners in Southern Baptist life. I invited them to join me in this venture. They were enthusiastic about the possibilities. From there we began.

We found the theory easier to write about than the practical aspects of ministry. It is within that painful tension that this book can be most helpful. Not only are we concerned with what happens to people; we are concerned with how we can minister to them more effectively.

Cos Davis brings his particular strength as a pastor for fifteen years, professor in preschool education for five years, and denominational worker in the preschool area. Cos is currently supervisor of the preschool program section, Sunday School Department, Baptist Sunday School Board.

Bruce Powers has served churches for twelve years in Kentucky, Georgia, and Florida. He served the denomination through the Baptist Sunday School Board for six years. Since 1978 he has been professor of Christian Education at Southeastern Baptist Theological Seminary.

Jim Minton is currently assistant professor of youth education at the

New Orleans Baptist Theological Seminary. Jim brings the experience of minister to youth and professor to this work.

Thom Meigs has served for five years as a pastor, five years as a chaplain, and six years a professor of pastoral care and psychology of religion. Thom brings special insight to the young adult years from these three areas.

George Gaston has spent most of his career in local church pastoral ministry. Holding pastorates in Texas and Louisiana has equipped him to speak to the practical ministry issues addressed in this book. George served for several years as assistant professor of pastoral ministry at Southwestern Baptist Theological Seminary. George is currently pastor of Willow Meadows Baptist Church, Houston, Texas.

Al Meiburg has had a distinguished career as pastor, college professor, chaplain, and now professor of pastoral theology at Southeastern Baptist Theological Seminary. Al has a particular interest in ministry to the aging that is evident in his chapter.

I have served as pastor in Georgia, Kentucky, Indiana, and Tennessee. Prior to assuming my position at the Baptist Sunday School Board, I was associate pastor at Saint Charles Avenue Baptist Church in New Orleans, Louisiana. I presently serve as a specialist in pastoral ministry, working in the areas of proclamation and pastoral care.

An effort was made to leave each contributor's style intact. Also, the contributors included a bibliography of additional resources not referred to in their chapters. No attempt has been made to avoid duplications because one minister might have a particular interest in adolescence and another in aging. Readers will notice that some writers use male pronouns in a generic sense.

This book is offered as a tool in ministry to persons who care for others. It will give you easy access to developmental theory and practical ministry ideas. The book focuses on appropriate pastoral care to persons. To that end we pray it is helpful.

James E. Hightower, Jr.
Nashville, Tennessee

Contents

1
The Preschool Years: Enjoying Dependency/ Developing Independency
Cos H. Davis, Jr.

Several years ago in a church I served as pastor, a young child drew a picture of me. The picture showed me standing behind the pulpit, gesturing with one hand in the air. I obviously was preaching! I was startled to think that young child's perception of me could be limited to the activity he saw me doing most often. But his experiences were limited, and as he got to know me in other relationships his perception broadened.

The same holds true of our perception of young children—preschoolers. Often our ideas about them are based on fragments of knowledge and experiences. As we learn more through reading, observing, and experience, our understanding of them increases. As our understanding of preschoolers grows, we will be able to minister to them more effectively.

This chapter is designed to help us broaden our understanding of preschoolers. We will consider: Why are preschool years considered as foundational? Can a preschooler learn about God? How do preschoolers learn? What are some basic needs of preschoolers? What are some practical ways a minister can relate to preschoolers?

Preschool Years Are Foundational

The first five years of life are highly significant to the rest of one's life. What a child learns and feels during this time, particularly about himself, will be foundational to the rest of his life. By the time a child has finished his fifth year, he will have a pretty good idea as to his worth to parents and other important people such as teachers. He will also have acquired some basic feelings about what parents believe is important. If a child can be helped to feel good about himself, a good foundation for relationship with others can be built.

During the preschool years we have an excellent opportunity to lay foundations for the child's spiritual life. These foundations are important for Christian conversion and spiritual growth. Good learning experiences at church can help parents lay foundations for the child's spiritual growth. Our denomination provides excellent curriculum materials for preschool teachers.[1] The curriculum has teaching units based on concepts related to God, Jesus, natural world, church, Bible, self, others, and family.

Christian conversion and growth do not happen in a vacuum. The person who makes a willful choice to receive Christ as Savior does so out of a background of experiences which have prepared him for this decision. The better job we do in the preschool years, the better the child will be able to relate positively to God.

Men and women who teach preschoolers in our churches are doing important work! They, along with parents, are building the foundation necessary for Christian conversion and growth. There is a real sense in which a preschool teacher has been just as involved in a person's conversion as the Children's, Youth, or Adult teacher who actually leads him to accept Christ at a later time. Paul wrote in 1 Corinthians 3:6, "I planted, Apollos watered, but God was giving the increase" (NASB).[2]

The Needs of a Preschooler

Your work with people has proven that they act or react according to some need in their life. Often people with whom you work do not know why they do what they do or say what they say. A need, though unrecognized, still clamors for attention. God has made us with certain needs—some of which can be met only in relation to other persons.

Preschoolers have needs too. Understanding what those needs are and how to meet them will enable you to minister more effectively to the child and, in turn, help parents and teachers meet his needs.

Love.—Love is the most basic need of the preschooler. He senses he is loved as adults express gentleness and patience in relation to his physical needs and his inability to do many things for himself. Loving a preschooler means doing what is best for him. Loving him means understanding him enough to know what is best and being willing and unselfish enough to meet his needs. Proverbs 22:6 says, "Train up a child in the way he should go: and when he is old, he will not depart from it." Loving a child means taking responsibility to guide his life in ways which will help him be a well-adjusted, contributing member of society and servant of God. The attitude of such love is expressed in the words of Sybil Waldrop, "Every child needs 'someone who is just crazy about him.' "3

Self-worth.—Every preschooler needs to know that he is of worth to people who are important to him. He learns to value himself only as those closest to him treat him as a person of worth. If this need is satisfied, he will learn that others are of worth too. The child's future, in terms of relationships, basically hinges on whether or not he feels he is important to significant people. Such a sense of self-worth is not taught through a relentless barrage of gifts or the absence of rules or regulations but by the kind of love which deals patiently and purposefully with the needs of the child.

Acceptance.—Love is expressed and self-worth is taught as a preschooler senses that he is accepted by significant adults. Each child needs to know he is wanted and deeply appreciated by others. Parents must consciously attempt to instill the feeling that they are proud of him and that he does not have to do anything to be loved. He is loved because of who he is, not because of what he does! Before the child is born, parents need to be helped to accept the child as a gift from God and be happy if the Lord gives them a daughter instead of a son or vice versa.

Trust.—Preschoolers are almost totally dependent on adults to meet the basic physical, emotional, social, and spiritual needs of their lives. The baby learns trust by the way he is cared for—if his hunger and comfort needs are met in a loving manner. Every young child needs to be assured through experience that he can depend on parents and teachers to meet his needs and do what is best for him. The words "Johnny, I love you" are confusing to Johnny if his parents or teachers say the words but do not meet his needs.

The sense of trust which a young child can experience is the foundation for faith in God. Without trust relationships with significant adults faith in God is more difficult. There are several biblical references of Jesus' use of family relationships to describe the believer's relationship to God. (Matt. 5:9; 6:6,8-9; 7:8-11). Such verses emphasize that appropriate trusting relationships with the Heavenly Father are fostered in the context of trusting relationships in the earthly home!

Security.—Preschoolers need to feel safe. Apart from proper care, they can get into some dangerous situations. They may put something unsafe in their mouth or try to put the end of an object in an electrical socket. They may climb on top of a table or chair. They need adults who will recognize the limitations of their judgment and will do whatever is necessary to keep them as safe as possible.

Parents and teachers who set limits to protect the preschooler are building his sense of security as well as his appreciation for some rules. However, caution should be used so as not to stifle every attempt of the preschooler to do something new. Also, judgment should be used so as not to protect the child from minor scrapes which come as a part of normal play activities. If the parent or teacher is too protective, the preschooler will feel scared to try anything new! Balance is the key!

Guidance.—Preschoolers do not come with an understanding of how to get along in a world of people and things. This means they must be taught by parents and teachers. Guidance for the preschooler should involve the following: (1) teaching the child the proper use of toys and other objects without hurting himself or others or destroying the object; (2) teaching the child, at his own pace, to gradually become more concerned for the rights and needs of others. This is quite difficult with the young child who focuses primarily on his own needs. However, by the fourth or fifth year the preschooler should be able to play cooperatively with others and "take turns" in the use of toys. Meeting other needs related to self-image and love helps free the child to be more cooperative and focus less on what he wants.

Independence.—The growing preschooler must feel an increasing sense of being able to do some things on his own. He needs to develop a sense of independence in the things he is capable of doing. Of course, some things are well beyond his limits mentally and physically. Parents and teachers need to be aware of the child's limitation so as not to frustrate him with a task which is too difficult. To be able to do this one must understand that preschoolers are not "little adults" and cannot do or understand many adult things. However, there are many things a preschooler can do, and wants to do, for himself and should be allowed to do so.

How a Preschooler Thinks

Several years ago while teaching a seminary course on child development, a student told how his son had come home from school without his cap. The father threatened him by saying, "If you do that again, I'll knock your head off!" The next day his son came home with two caps—his and someone else's! This story illustrates some of the characteristics of thinking of young children—they take you literally for what you say, and morals do not seem to influence their conscious thought.

Literal Minded.—It is often amusing to get the interpretation of the mature five-year-old's understanding of what we say. On a trip with my family I called my five-year-old daughter's attention to a huge bridge up ahead by saying, "Kristen, we're going over that bridge in a little while." Her reaction was unusual excitement—she could hardly believe it! When we crossed the bridge she expressed her disappointment by complaining, "Daddy, we didn't go over that bridge." She had understood me literally to say we were going over the top of the bridge!

This limitation of literal-mindedness often causes confusion to the young child and should alert us to speak in more precise terms. While we cannot divest ourselves of all the "language of Zion," some terminology is particularly confusing to the young child. Remember how the literal-minded child thinks when he hears such statements as "Jesus lives in my heart" or the words of favorite hymns like "There Is a Fountain Filled with Blood"!

Here and Now.—The preschooler is limited to what is in the here and now. If you ask a five-year-old to describe God, he may (if he is at that stage of capability) draw you a very large stick person! As adults we realize that God is spirit (John 4:24) and cannot be adequately described in human terms. But preschoolers have no concept of spirit and describe everything according to their experience. For example, a preschooler who has seen only a blue ball may not think that a ball can be red. Therefore, the red ball is not a ball to him! He must be told that it is.

Short Attention Span.—One of the most frustrating things about preschoolers to most adults is their inability to pay attention for an extended period of time. This is one reason why preschoolers learn best through a variety of activities which take only a little time in which to participate. The parent or teacher who insists on a two-year-old sitting still for five minutes while they tell a long Bible story will not have an audience after about one minute or so! Therefore, teaching activities and materials must be designed with consideration for the short attention span limitation of preschoolers.

Shallow Learner.—Preschoolers also tend to be interested only in the shallow or surface facts of an object or story. They cannot deal with the subtle meanings or implications of a story such as the "Good Samaritan." Only the simplest facts can be related. Likewise a child looking at a nature object may be impressed with only the color and size of the object while seeming unconcerned with other characteristics. This is why it is important not to expect a preschooler to be able to deal with much detail or intricate facts. The preschooler must be exposed to the same object, song, or story many times before he will tire of it. Why? Because as a shallow learner he is gradually understanding more and more through repeated exposures.

Saying and Understanding.—One final point needs to be made relative to the thinking of the preschooler. He can say many things he does not understand. His physical ability to say complicated words or words with religious significance may be far advanced of his ability to understand what he is saying. For example, a child can be taught to say, "Jesus lives in my heart" and that sounds religious and spiritual. But, does the preschooler really understand the truth of that statement? Can a preschooler really put that truth to use? We must not assume that saying something spiritual means the preschooler has understood what the word or phrase means.

The Preschooler's Developmental Tasks

During the first six years of life an individual is confronted with three basic psycho-social tasks. Erik Erikson[4] has identified these developmental tasks as trust, autonomy, and initiative.

If these tasks are not begun at the proper time, it is doubtful if the person will make the proper life adjustments at other stages of his life. For example, the developmental tasks of adolescence and adulthood are related to those of the earliest years. Should a person be deficient in trust, autonomy, and initiative, his psycho-social growth at later stages would be adversely affected.

Now, let's overview the developmental tasks of preschoolers in order to show the importance of each one. Each task will be discussed with a general time frame in focus although every child will not fit this time frame precisely because of differences in physical, emotional, and mental maturation.

Trust

Trust is the first and most basic developmental task in life. Trust is learning to rely on others for needs to be met. It is learning the feeling of security and well-being about your relationship with significant others.

This task has its roots in the first two years of life when the child is most dependent. It arises out of the fact that almost everything must be done for the young child during this time—he is almost totally dependent! He cannot feed himself, change himself when wet or soiled, bathe himself, cover himself when cold. These are the concerns of the parent or other caregiver. If the child learns that others are going to take care of him, he can "relax" and trust himself to them. If his basic needs are met in a loving way, the young child will develop a basic sense of trust.

Autonomy

Some refer to autonomy as that stage of understanding that you are a person apart from others. You have a self of your own. You are independent of others. This task is dependent on trust and is focused in the two- and three-year-old child. Autonomy is often expressed in many types of independent actions.

During the first two years of life the child is gradually developing skills which will make him less dependent on an adult to do many things for him. By around one year he is beginning to walk, and by eighteen months or so he is beginning to talk. These skills are pretty well developing by the time a child reaches two. These skills will be further refined by the time he reaches his fourth birthday. So will feeding himself and toilet training.

Perhaps you have heard a parent refer to her child as a "terrible two." The reference is usually to a child who is at the emotional stage of having a tantrum when he does not get his way or becomes frustrated with an activity. This is a normal expression for children who are trying to establish independence and are frustrated by the restraints of adults or by an activity that is too difficult for their abilities.

While the years of autonomy or independence can be trying for adults, all is not negative. These are years of learning for the child, years of testing his skills, years of gaining confidence. He is growing and feels safe enough to try out new things on his own. Parents who will deal patiently with their child during this difficult stage will see emerge a more confident and self-assured individual.

Initiative

The four- or five-year-old is at the age when initiative becomes important. While the twos or threes expressed independence within their limited abilities, fours and fives have highly developed abilities and use their imagination quite well.

Fours and fives act upon their environment to change it. Give a five-year-old a set of wooden blocks and he may build a house with doors and windows! His imagination is active and he uses it to draw, or paint, or in other creative expressions. While he still mixes fantasy and reality, his initiative finds expression in some form.

During this stage he needs lots of opportunities to express himself through music, art, stories, blocks, homeliving materials, and so forth. He is totally involved and approaches his work with intensity and abandon!

Can a Preschooler Learn About God?

What an important question for a pastor or minister of education! The answer to this question has all kinds of interesting implications about whether to provide "baby-sitting" or planned learning experiences while preschoolers are at church. The answer to this question also has implications related to whether just "anybody" can work with preschoolers or whether we need knowledgeable, trained people to teach them. This question also opens for consideration the provision of well-equipped rooms, adequate amount of space, and learning materials appropriate for preschoolers.

To say that preschoolers are interested in learning is an understatement. They are consumed by the need to learn. They investigate almost anything that will stand still for an examination! You have heard the relentless barrage of questions about what? why? who? You have been amazed at their untiring energy as they have gone from one activity to another and then to another. What is all this ceaseless activity about? Why this compulsion to get on with living? LEARNING! Preschoolers are learners. They are acquiring bits and pieces of ideas that will later become concepts. They are acquiring feelings that they will later associate with facts. To say that a preschooler cannot learn would be nonsense. We know they learn.

But can preschoolers learn about God? Can foundational feelings and ideas be taught as building blocks for later years? Should we wait until later elementary years to begin teaching children about God?

Avenues of Learning

Preschoolers can learn about God. God wants to make Himself known to the young as well as to those who are older through whatever means they can know Him. The following are tested avenues through which preschoolers learn about God.

Relationship with Significant People.—People such as parents, family members, and teachers provide the most important avenue through which preschoolers learn. The value of positive relationships is incalculable to the preschooler's feeling of his personal value. Through relationships he learns about his self-worth as love is provided or withheld. He learns values as they are modeled by significant adults. In essence, his whole outlook on life and his concept of God are influenced by people who are important to him. His feeling about being loved and accepted by God is greatly dependent on whether or not he feels this love and acceptance from those who mean most to him.

Senses.—God made us with five senses. The preschoolers use all of these for learning. Through hearing, smelling, seeing, tasting, and touching a young child becomes familiar with the world God has made. These physical gifts are the preschooler's way of dealing with the world around him and offer an excellent opportunity to teach the child about God and his care for them.

Repetition.—Unlike adults, preschoolers do not tire easily of seeing or hearing the same thing over and over again. The fifth time the story is told can hold as much joy and excitement for the preschooler as the first. Why do preschoolers never seem to tire of the same story or song? He learns from repetition. Hearing or seeing something repeated gives him opportunity to build on previous experiences. Little by little, through repetition, the preschooler learns more about God and the people and things God has made.

Play.—Preschoolers also learn through what we adults refer to as "play." Play is not a useless activity—it is a child's work. Play is his business. Through play he is learning about people and things in his world. He uses his imagination as he plays out the role of a policeman, nurse, father, mother, or a number of other persons. Through play he experiments with ideas and gains confidence in himself and his abilities. The play or activity learning approach by preschool teachers allows learning to proceed from the needs and interests of the child rather than imposing "learning" that is not of interest to him.

Doing.—Preschoolers are doers. They learn through participating. They are active and involved. Understanding what a child is capable of doing frees the teacher to allow the child to do what he can for himself. Doing and accomplishing tasks build the child's confidence and independence. Such confidence will encourage him to participate in other activities in which he can learn about God.

Imitating.—Preschoolers also learn by doing what they see others do. Parents and teachers can often be embarrassed as they observe a preschooler repeat their actions or words. The fact that preschoolers learn by imitation should serve as a caution to those who teach them to exhibit positive actions and words.

Curiosity.—The hunger to know leads the preschooler to explore what is unknown to him. Curiosity prompts him to smell, taste, and touch almost any object. He is most happy when a variety of materials is supplied for him to explore. The preschooler's natural desire to learn provides the teacher an unbelievable opportunity to teach about God and the things He made.

Satisfaction.—The preschooler learns to have positive feelings and attitudes about church if he has satisfying experiences in what he is doing. Satisfaction comes when he is able to complete a task within his range of ability or to have positive, affirming relationships with teachers and a growing degree of competence in relating to other preschoolers. The preschool teacher should plan so that each child in the department will have satisfying experiences each session.

The Bible and Preschoolers

One of the major concerns of the church is to teach the Bible to all who will avail themselves of the opportunity to learn about God's revelation through Scripture. The Bible is a book for all ages: preschool, children, youth, and adults. Preschoolers can learn some important biblical concepts which are foundational to those he should learn at a later age. For this reason, those who teach preschoolers are not "baby-sitting" or entertaining preschoolers while everyone else is learning about the Bible. Preschool teachers "teach" preschoolers about the Bible.

An important consideration in teaching preschoolers the Bible is to teach it on their level of understanding. Biblical truth must be simplified and communicated in ways which preschoolers learn best. For example, singing "God made the flower, Thank you, God" to a preschooler who is examining a flower communicates a biblical truth about creation. This is an appropriate approach but is far less complicated than discussing the stewardship implications of Genesis 1 with a group of adults. Both the preschooler and adults are being taught at their own level of understanding. What the preschooler is being taught (that God made the world for our benefit) is absolutely foundational to the idea of stewardship which the adult is being taught!

Biblical Concepts for Preschoolers

There are eight concept areas under which most preschool educators categorize what preschoolers can learn about the Bible. These concept areas are listed below with a general statement about what we hope preschoolers will learn.[5]

God.—We want preschoolers to have positive feelings about people and things associated with God. We want them to associate the created world with God.

Jesus.—We want preschoolers to sense that Jesus was born, grew, belonged to a family, and was a very special person.

Natural World.—Our aim is to teach preschoolers that God made the world good and beautiful and that "thank you, God" is an appropriate response.

Bible.—We want to help preschoolers think of the Bible as a special book which tells about God and Jesus.

Self.—The biblical view of the importance of oneself should be communicated to preschoolers. Personal relationships, environment and Bible-related activities can enhance the child's appreciation of himself as a person of worth.

Others.—Preschool teachers try to help preschoolers become more aware that others are important, too. With proper guidance, the preschooler should begin to act and respond to others in appropriate ways.

Family.—We desire to help preschoolers become more aware that God planned for families and to learn some ways in which families are special to them.

Church.—We want preschoolers to have good experiences at church and to have positive feelings about church.

How You Can Minister to Preschoolers

There are many things you can do personally and through others to minister to the preschoolers who are part of your congregation. The following are some practical suggestions related to the information already shared on the development and needs of preschoolers.

Maximize Opportunities of Foundational Years

As the leader of your church you have an excellent opportunity to influence parents, teachers and, church committees regarding the importance of foundational years.

Influence teachers and appropriate committees to determine definite goals for teaching preschoolers.—Working with appropriate preschool materials, committees can determine definite educational goals for each preschool stage and age. This work is usually assigned to the Preschool Committee. Teachers can receive specific training related to readiness levels of the children they teach and how to determine goals for them.

Use foundational years to relate to God's plan for conversion and Christian growth.—Use every opportunity you have to help teachers and educational committees see that God wants teachers and parents to become partners in His redemptive purpose. Parents and teachers can be led to see that the foundational years can be used as part of the process of conversion and Christian growth. The preschool years are the time for building trust which can become the foundation for saving faith at a later time.

Provide a person who understands preschoolers and is competent in planning for preschoolers, parents, and teachers.—Your church may need to desig-nate a person (staff or volunteer) who will be responsible for planning overall programs for preschoolers. The quality of programs for pre-schoolers and their parents can be improved greatly when a person is specifically assigned to that work.

Preach sermons and offer seminars on the importance of the foundational years.—Sermons can be prepared so that information related to the importance of the preschool years can be shared. When appropriate, occasional references to young children will communicate your love for young children and support for work related to them.

Be a supporter of preschool work.—One of the most helpful things you can do is to have a positive attitude toward preschoolers, parents, and the ministry of the church related to them. An occasional supportive word about certain planned events, a verbal pat on the back to pre-school workers, and an interest in what is happening will communicate that you are a friend to preschool work.

Provide Training for Understanding Preschoolers' Needs

Many parents would be receptive to a seminar designed to help them understand and meet the needs of their preschoolers. The church needs to offer help in this area because so little of what they can read on their own is dealt with in a Christian context. Needs of preschoolers should be part of the basic content of the ongoing training program for all preschool teachers. Teachers must start with the child and his needs in order to be an effective teacher.

Be Aware of How Preschoolers Think

The fact that preschoolers are literal, concrete, and shallow in their thinking has some important implications for you. What can be done to recognize this reality?

Prepare worship services with some consideration for preschoolers.—Make a definite attempt to communicate with the young child through a ser-mon illustration they will understand. Occasionally choose music they can sing. Provide a children's sermon or Bible story during the worship time.

Keep teaching concepts at an appropriate level.—Avoid being pressured by parents and others for teachers to teach concepts that are inappropri-ate for them. The earlier statement about teaching goals related to preschoolers should be considered. Remember that because a concept is biblical is not justification for attempting to teach it to a preschooler. There are two tests for what to teach preschoolers: (1) Is it biblical? (2) Is it appropriate for a preschooler?

The suggestions which follow are purely personal—things you can do with a preschooler to help him feel he is important to you.

Eyeball to Eyeball.—As adults we have difficulty realizing how frustrating it must be to relate to people when we can only talk to their knee caps. Get the point? You will greatly improve the preschooler's appreciation for you, and yours for him, if you bend down to talk with him on his eye level. Look in his eyes, smile and say something like, "Johnny, I'm glad you're at church today." This brief contact will make a real difference in how children and their parents perceive you. If you really want to be brave and have the time, ask parents to be sure that you get to greet the children as they leave the worship service.

Get to Know Preschoolers.—Many pastors and staff persons spend lots of time getting to know the names, hobbies, and other facts of adult members. What about getting to know the names of preschoolers so that you can call thier names when you talk with them? You might want to ask parents to make a name tag for their child to wear if you decide to greet them on a certain Sunday. This can be done several times until you have learned all their names.

Be Aware of Preschoolers.—As you walk about in the church or visit in a home be aware of preschoolers. Be available to them and become the friend of as many as will let you. Be conscious of opportunities to challenge their curiosity by calling attention to the feel and smell of the flower you are wearing or listening to the sound of your watch.

Be "huggable."—You are a figure of authority to preschoolers, and many may be afraid of you at first. But as you open your life to them they will love you for the warm, gentle person they are able to experience you as being. One of the greatest treats for them and you is that you allow them to hug you and feel your embrace in return.

Notes

1. Materials provided for Sunday School, Church Training, Missions, and Music.

2. From the *New American Standard Bible.* Copyright © The Lockman Foundation, 1960, 1962, 1963, 1968, 1971, 1972, 1973, 1975, 1977. Used by permission.

3. C. Sybil Waldrop, *Understanding Today's Preschoolers* (Nashville: Convention Press, 1982), p. 48.

4. See Anne Hitchcock Gilliland, *Understanding Preschoolers* (Nashville: Convention Press, 1969), p. 55.

5. Adapted from the leaflet *How a Preschooler Learns About God* by Cos H. Davis (Nashville: The Sunday School Board of the Southern Baptist Convention, 1982).

Additional Bibliography

Castle, Leon. *A Year of Children's Sermons.* Nashville: Broadman Press, 1976.
Davis, Cos H. *Children and the Christian Faith.* Nashville: Broadman Press, 1979.

2
The Early School Years: Finding Acceptance Beyond the Family
Bruce P. Powers

Most ministers take for granted the religious development of children. Consider congregations you know. Pastors typically spend about 90 percent of their time on worship, education, counseling, and administration concerns that focus primarily on adults. Very little time is devoted to *direct* involvement with children and to activities that will assist parents as they influence the religious development of their children.

The problem with this is that the greatest potential for influencing Christian development is not with adolescents or adults but with children and preschoolers. With preschoolers it is the loving, Christian nurture that has greatest impact. With children it is the living example of their primary caregivers and the direct religious instruction—which gives guidance about beliefs and practices—that have the greatest influence.

So the role of the minister in caring for children is really twofold: how to relate to children and how to help parents relate to their children. Only when a minister is actively involved in both is a holistic concept of care for children being practiced.[1]

Focus on Ages Six Through Twelve

This chapter deals specifically with the early school years, grades one through six (roughly ages 6-12). It is written to assist ministers and other interested persons in dealing *directly* with the needs and concerns of these children so as to foster their spiritual, emotional, and intellectual development.

In the first part of the chapter I will describe the growth of children ages six through twelve, give characteristics of their spiritual, emotional, and intellectual development, and illustrate symptoms calling for an

25

informed response by ministers, teachers, parents, or other caring persons.

In the latter portion, I will focus more on the practical side of working with children, both directly and through the parents.

As you saw in the previous chapter, the initial impressions gained during preschool years are major imprints for subsequent phases of development. Growth occurs as a child successfully integrates and transforms the various facets of his or her life based on *previous* imprints and *current* reality. The information which follows builds on the premise that a child is physically and mentally capable of achieving the transformations usually expected between ages six and twelve. Although wide differences are to be expected among children—and symptoms and interventions regarding a wide range of behavior will be mentioned—the material presented will not necessarily be applicable to children with obvious physical and psychological problems. In such cases, consult with or refer parents to a medical doctor or a child psychologist.

How a Child Develops

"My child is in the fourth grade and has trouble reading. She often confuses words like *was* and *saw*. And she says she is bored with all kinds of school, including Sunday School."

"Carson is in an unusual phase. He is always telling us things that are right and wrong about what we—*his parents*—do. Can you imagine a child nine years old acting that way?"

"Janet is only eleven, but she is a full foot taller than many of the girls *and* boys her age. Her body is developing, but she is still a kid. Is this normal?"

"My twelve-year-old grandson used to be so smart. He could tell me all kinds of interesting things about nature, history, and even about the books of the Bible. Now, even when I can get him to talk about what he is learning, he just says, 'Nothing much, Grandma.' "

You can probably identify with some of these statements; they represent the *usual* rather than the unusual in our relations with children. Perhaps a good question is: What should we expect from children as they develop?

From experience we know that there is a great capacity for facts and for using information in solving problems. And we also observe that somehow children develop skills in *using* their knowledge as they solve arithmetic problems, tell time, select clothes to wear, write letters, and play games many adults cannot even understand. (Look at the children who can use a computer!)

Along with the intellectual development, there is steady growth of the body and ability to control it. Growth seems to come in spurts, and during the latter half of this age range the girls surpass the boys in physical development.

Younger children must be active; they get restless when their bodies must be still. By middle childhood, however, they begin to develop the use of smaller muscles and the concentration that allow for longer periods of intense work and play. Physical skills, coordination, and endurance are the major developments by late childhood.

Emotionally, the child's major adjustment is identifying the authorities in his or her life. During preschool years, those who counted were the parents, or caregivers. Upon moving into the larger world of school and community, a child must sort out those persons and things that really count. Associated with this change, the intellectual need to learn literally causes children to identify the people and places that give the answers or tell the rules. They then seek to gain approval or get attention by following or imitating their authorities. For most children, those persons and things that have the greatest exposure or the respect of family and friends will most likely be viewed as authoritative in a child's mind. During the latter years of childhood, peers become more and more influential, gradually assuming a role of major authority during adolescence.

Socially, around eight years there is the possibility of a child feeling inferior to others as he or she recognizes an inability to perform like older children. About ten, the social interests of boys and girls begin to diverge widely as they begin to gather in cliques and boys focus on boy-things and girls focus on girl-things.

Changes from Age Six Through Twelve

With this general overview, let me now take you through the experiences of one child so that you can see the subtle transformations. I will focus on the intellectual development, as this is the center for processing the whole of a child's experience. Physical developments are fairly well known; but psychological innerworkings are not well understood and represent a key area for improvement in providing care for children. Think of the children you know as I describe some of the typical changes in the life of a child.

Jason is our typical child. Prior to entering first grade his mental work consisted primarily of making relationships between *experience* and *action*. For example, he learned the connection between asking for a glass of milk and receiving it, bad behavior and punishment, hunger and eating, and the rules about day and night, hot and cold, happy and sad. These are very *simple* thoughts to the young child; he does not *create* and use these ideas at will to get his way. Rather they are a direct response to a stimulus that the child identifies—thus Jason makes a connection. There is nothing thought-out about this activity. Jason simply tells or does as he perceives the situation.

Around the sixth year, Jason begins to make multiple connections. He gradually gains the capacity to manipulate or rework information. This information is organized in unique patterns that become important to the child; and the child develops the ability to draw selectively from the material to answer questions and solve problems. Thus *before* age six, Jason wanted all of his toys; he did not like the idea of sharing if *he* wanted an item. Now he is learning that sharing can create friends, and that if he shares, others will share with him. Much social experience, integrated with the basic information for living, are the major social developments during the first two years.

Of all the intellectual and social developments during this age, the most important of these is reading. Usually learning to read is a natural act for most children but does not come to all at the same time. In most cases, a child has a *eureka!* moment when there is recognition of a written word. This insight cannot be forced on a child, but can be encouraged by exposure to the many different aids that teachers use to help children find the key, such as letter and picture flashcards. (Children learn to read by stringing the sounds of letters togethers. The *eureka!* moment comes when a child sounds out all the letters in a word and realizes that it is the same word that he or she already uses in conversation. For one of our children, the word was *cab.* He saw a taxi stopped at a light and made the sounds, kuh-a-buh. He said it again slowly, then shouted, "Cab! That's a *cab.*")

Of all the mental developments during the early childhood years, rote memory increases the most. Attention span increases so that the child can be interested in a continuing story from day to day whereas previously everything was done in single episodes. Work, reading, and play sessions become longer, and there is an obvious effort to continue or get back to uncompleted tasks that were enjoyable.

During middle childhood (ages 8-10), the greatest growth is in reading. The ability to substitute symbols for actions is a marvelous achievement that allows Jason to roam the world of adventure through the written word. He also is a master of information—facts. He knows reasons for everything, can tell you why he is right and you are wrong, and will argue over the rules of a game he is playing as much as he will play the game.

Usually during the tenth year there will be a reading explosion. Parents will watch with awe as children read dozens of books. In some cases, parents take this as a clue that the child is gifted and they begin to arrange special educational opportunities. In other cases, parents try to redirect the child's interest to more active pursuits such as recreation, housekeeping, and even homework activities. This reading indulgence is to be expected; it is perfectly normal. Let Jason enjoy the new expanded world that reading provides. In most instances, this extensive reading is *not* giftedness and is *not* an escape from responsibility; it is simply the *right* expression for the child's phase of development. There will be a gradual decline in reading time so that by age thirteen Jason will have to be encouraged to read rather than spend large amounts of time listening to music or playing videogames.

Jason's imagination develops rapidly during middle childhood, enriching the adventures he has through reading. He actually *is* the space pilot, the detective, the mom or dad he is imitating. *Make-believe* becomes a very real game, and he wants you to act with him as if he were that person. Play characters soon give way, however, to acting out adventures. For boys, this is usually action-oriented such as exploring and space-fighters. For girls, it can be action *and* activities such as homemaking or acting like a television personality. For both sexes, they identify *heroes*—both real and fictional—whom they imitate.

Don't worry about the child's trips of fantasy. They are fun experiences that allow the real to interact with the larger world that the child is coming to know. As intellectual growth continues, the real world wins, and children gradually lose the beautiful capacity to transcend the ordinary. One caution, however. If Jason increasingly lives in imaginary experiences and does not appear able to *separate* the real and the unreal, consult a physician for advice. By age twelve, a child should spend most of his or her time in the real world.

Middle childhood is also the time for the flowering of artistic and athletic talent. Such expressions are not polished, mind you, but they are observable and can be encouraged through group and individual lessons.

As Jason becomes an older child, his intelligence approaches maturity. His rote memory and arithmetical reasoning are almost at their peak; as he grows older, he will simply enrich and build on the basic skills acquired by this period. By the end of this phase, he will have learned a massive amount of information, such as the multiplication tables, names of the United States and their capitals, and the names and categories of living things. (In our family, one of the important accomplishments is memorizing the books of the Bible and being able to tell basic Christian beliefs.)

Rote memory and logical thinking are major strengths of older children, but this does not mean that the child can do *abstract* and *philosophical* reasoning like an adult; these are the mental operations that are *developing* during this phase. Jason learns to ask and pose answers to the *what if?* questions; he poses alternatives and considers options. He develops a little bit of the adult's suspicion, and becomes aware that everything isn't exactly as it appears. For example, sleight-of-hand magic can enthrall younger children; but the older child begins to look for the trick. At the *beginning* of this phase, Jason would reason: *After a rain, the grass is wet. The grass is wet this morning; therefore it rained.* By the *end*, he would observe the wet grass and think: *Did it rain? Or did Dad turn on the sprinkler? Or is that dew on the front lawn?* Mental operations that originally were limited to the concrete (I-see-it-therefore-it-is) type of thinking enlarge to include abstract, or conjecture-thinking (when you consider possibilities).

Another major development is an enlargement of the artistic and athletic control functions in the brain. These special aptitudes can emerge in remarkable ways in later childhood. Adults need to be alert to special interests of children so as to cultivate their development whenever possible. But be careful not to impose *adult* or *parental* ambitions on children; they must develop what God has given *them*.

During the two years prior to adolescence, Jason has experienced a slowing down of the rapid growth he had earlier. This creates some problems, since girls during this time continue to grow and for a year or two surpass boys of the same age. Children are able to learn complex motor skills, and often will devote a great deal of time to developing both individual and team skills. With this development, the competetive spirit becomes a major influence in a child's activity.

These physical developments blend with the emotional changes that occur prior to adolescence. There is great variety among the activities of older children as each seeks to find others who have similar interests and compatible needs. Feeling good about oneself, achieving a sense of independence, and acceptance among peers are the focal concerns, and obviously are interrelated. This leads usually to a few close playmates, who may view themselves as a special group or club. Competition is handled by seeking those who are like you or who will accept you; thus there are three general patterns that help children cope with this need: a close-knit group of boys, a close-knit group of girls, and the loner (persons who cannot find others with similar interests and needs, or who for some reason do not find fulfillment in competing with others. An example is a child who continues to lose himself or herself in reading or other indoor activity to the exclusion of group play.)

Childhood ends with a blend of adventure, competition, physical well-being, and a strong sense of self-reliance. The child during these years has dealt with three major spheres of development:

- Integration of the rather limited experiences of family and home with the larger sphere of peer and community influences.
- Development of logical processes that enable a person to move from concrete to abstract thinking—to function in the realm of adult concepts and communication.
- Development of physical skills that allow one to compete in individual and team activities.

The Child and Faith Development

How the child develops religious concepts can be inferred from the information given above, but for reference, here is a nutshell summary.

Prior to age six, religious concepts are primarily intuitive, and come from participation in and observation of the faith experiences of their caregivers. During childhood years, there is a gradual move to take part in and adopt for oneself the stories, beliefs, and practices which are a part of the child's family and church.

These religious concepts are absorbed through informal exposure as well as through intentional, structured experiences. Learning focuses on literal interpretations, with distinct rules for judging right and wrong, good and bad. Authority is very important, and conformity—doing things like they are supposed to be done—is a virture. Peer pressure is not an issue for the child as it is for an adolescent.

At the beginning of this phase, the child must learn to be a participant —learn how to be accepted and feel secure. By ten or eleven, the child will have developed authoritative rules, reasons, and answers to categorize his or her faith. In many ways, these concepts are a composite of the informal and formal religious impressions which the child has assimilated and codified. Literal interpretation of the Bible and any other *authority* source such as a book, television program, preacher, teacher, or policeman is to be expected during this age.

Approaching puberty, faith concepts of peers become increasingly important; the molding influence of significant persons and groups with whom the child-youth identifies begins to substitute for the authorities accepted earlier. This peer orientation usually becomes evident at about twelve, and can be a dominant influence throughout life. At this point, persons pattern their lives according to the norms expressed by those who are important to and accepting of them. Beliefs and practices may be highly consistent with those experienced earlier, or they may represent a radical departure, depending on the significant others one chooses.[2]

Tasks to Be Accomplished

You now have the basic developmental pattern that might be expected in children. To summarize, it would be helpful to recall the developmental tasks associated with childhood. You may remember that the necessity of achieving certain tasks during each age period was first proposed by Robert Havighurst.[3]

These tasks grow out of the three spheres of development mentioned earlier. They represent the achievements needed to enable persons to adjust successfully at their current age and prepare them to progress satisfactorily into the next phase of life.

Although these tasks have been enlarged and interpreted in a variety of ways, the basic need for children to achieve certain competencies as proposed by Havighurst remains. A working knowledge of these is helpful in order to assess the developmental issues operating in the life of a child as well as diagnosing areas of deficiency in those entering puberty.

For your information and reference, they are listed in figure 1.

FIGURE 1

Tasks to Be Accomplished During Childhood[4]

In order to adjust successfully and in order to prepare for the next phase of life, a child entering puberty should have accomplished the following at a level appropriate for the society in which he or she lives.

1. Physical skills necessary for ordinary games.
2. Wholesome attitudes toward oneself as a growing person.
3. Ability to get along with age-mates.
4. Appropriate masculine or feminine role identification.
5. Fundamental skills in reading, writing, and calculating.
6. Concepts and abstract thinking necessary for everyday living.
7. Conscience, morality, and a scale of values.
8. Personal independence.
9. Attitudes to facilitate social interaction in groups and within institutions.

Practical Dimensions

Let us turn now to the practical dimensions of relating to and understanding children, and information and guidelines that can be shared with parents and used by church ministers.

In caring for persons, there is no substitute for the quality of living and relationship that you share with those you are seeking to serve. This is true for all ages, but especially so for children; they are so indelibly influenced by example and by the treatment they receive from authority figures. What you do most of the time will have to come from a sense of rightness—giving and receiving, initiating and responding—based on the felt needs of any situation. This you must learn to do without developing a *game plan* based on formalized theories and techniques. This is the *informed* minister, caring for persons out of who and what you are.

However, there are times when specific information and strategies are required in order to develop one's personal skills, or to improve the total care provided within the life of a family, an age group in a church, or within a total congregation. Such information and actions are termed interventions—those preventive or prescriptive steps taken by a caregiver to direct or redirect the development of others in order to solve a real or potential problem.

The remainder of this chapter focuses on information and actions that can be used in both preventive and prescriptive ways with children and their parents. The material is not designed so much as a sequential teaching device as it is a reference section. As such, you can read it straight through, or you can simply turn to one of the topical headings for some concise information and/or guidelines which can be used.

The information may be directed toward ministers, but also relates directly to parents and other caring persons in a congregation. Each section is easily adaptable for use in relating to the age group or in assisting others in improving their caregiving.

A Child's Position in the Family

The information provided thus far is for children in general. Some will develop exactly as described; others will vary widely, even in the same family.

Of special significance according to many authorities are the changes that occur when there are two or more children in a family. Although there are many related influences such as gender of a child, role models, peers, and stability of home life, that might produce similar responses—the one *predictable* influence that is at the root of a great many pastoral care issues is a child's position among siblings.

Rudolf Dreikus and Loren Grey are two of the specialists who have provided helpful guidance on this topic. For over a decade they have been seeking to alert professionals to the major impact position in the family has on a child's development. Their book *A Parents' Guide to Child Discipline* was a central resource for preparing this section.[5]

The Oldest Child

The first child is the major attraction and thrives on being the central figure in the newly developed family triad. Being first and only (except in the case of multiple births, of course) the first child develops just as described earlier until a brother or sister is born. *Number One* is displaced, at least temporarily, and can experience this as rejection. Having had *all* the attention, he or she now has to seek a share of the parents' time.

If the age difference between the siblings is three or less, this cannot be explained to the older child. He or she must be given extra attention in order to keep from feeling rejected; if this is not done, the child will seek attention in whatever way possible.

Even up to age five the shock is rather extreme. But for this older child, an explanation is helpful. They can lovingly be guided into the joy of becoming one of the care persons for the newborn.

You will notice that, as a group, oldest children tend to be more conservative, to prefer authority—they like to give orders—and tend to dislike change. Since parents probably gave them more responsibility in early years, they tend to be better administrators and managers than those who were second and third children.

The Second Child

Although the first child is *displaced* as the single recipient of parental affection, the second child comes to view the situation differently. He or she sees the older sibling as the pacesetter, as the number one in terms of ability and in the attention received from parents. Consequently, the basic imprint for the second child is to equal and even pass the older child. If frustrated, the child will turn to behavior and/or pursuits that gain attention, usually either regressive and antisocial actions or activities in which the child can excell.

Research suggests that second children are usually much more flexible than first children and see change as a means of gaining power. They are much more likely to be creative, but are less consistent than first children in carrying out their ideas.[6]

The Middle Child

If a third child arrives, displacement must be added to the adjustment problems already faced by the second child. According to Dreikus and Grey, a middle child usually discovers that it is necessary not only to compete in one area with a sibling who is larger and stronger and more capable but must share his or her attention and affection with the new arrival.[7]

An obvious tension develops in middle children as they are seeking acceptance and affirmation. They feel pulled between being like the older sibling and being like the newborn. This becomes a basic question of identity, an issue which a middle child often will carry throughout life unless resolved early.

The basic need for a middle child, then, is affirmation as an individual. Equal time and caring from *parents,* not from an older sibling or other substitute, will help the child to resolve the identity crisis he or she feels.

The Youngest Child

The youngest child in a family has a unique advantage related to attention and parental affection. He or she is never displaced by a younger sibling. Although there may be extremes of behavior to secure *additional* attention, the youngest child never has to surrender the tolerance and laxity of parental demands accorded to the baby in a family.

Consequently, this child is often viewed as being spoiled, the one who needs to have his or her way, the one who needs to be cared for. In the extreme, this person gradually becomes overly dependent on others—a *leaner* in adulthood—or a manipulator, who seeks to get his or her needs met without considering the impact on others.

Due probably to the great ambiguity perceived by the youngest child in the values and practices within his or her family—this child grows up trying to make sense of a myriad of social, emotional, and intellectual stimuli coming from mother, father, and all the sibling parent-figures —the youngest is the most likely child to break with the patterns of belief and practice held by the parents. An example of this is the child who chooses an occupation or follows a style of living in which the personality characteristics or activities run counter to the prevailing family pattern.[8]

The Only Child

This child is never displaced, but never has one close in age or capability with whom to interact. Therefore the only child must orient himself or herself entirely to the parents.

The only child may display some of the characteristics of the youngest child, but this seems to be influenced largely by how the parents treat the child—most often seen are the only children who are raised and cared for as babes regardless of age, and those who are brought up as little adults.

Although it usually takes the only child longer to develop the skills to relate socially with peers, "this does not appear to affect significantly [one's] ability to adjust to the world as an adult."9

The Family as a System

It is easy to see that the family is not just a collection of individuals, and that it is not simply a composite of its members. Rather, it is, as often referred to in family counseling literature and workshops, a *system.* There are no simple answers and no pat interventions that will guarantee success for parents, teachers, and others who work with the family. The reason is this: *whatever happens in any part of the interrelated family system ultimately influences and is influenced by every other part.*

The best we can do, therefore, is to seek the best understanding possible, and to develop consistent practices based on principles and guidelines that are consistent with Christian ideals and personal conscience.

The material included in this chapter assumes some awareness of the family as system. The developmental issues which have been presented, as well as the practical suggestions which follow, require that they be viewed from an holistic perspective. To treat one action or one event in pastoral care without getting in touch with the larger context is like a physician treating a symptom rather than seeking the cause of the symptom.10 So it must be with those who are seeking to provide care and nurture for children in a Christian setting. The need is threefold:

- Be informed about the developmental needs of children.
- Provide care and counsel with an awareness of the larger system within which the child lives.
- Know your limitations; refer cases to appropriate child and family

care specialists when you are unsure of or unable to provide the care required.

Reward and Punishment

Why do kids do what they do? Behavior is shaped by its consequences—by the reward and/or punishment received. If you would like to see more of certain behaviors, you have to reward the child for engaging in those actions.

If, however, you would like to see less of a certain behavior, you can do one or both of two things:

- Punish the child when the undesired behavior is exhibited.
- Remove the rewards which have served to maintain the undesired behavior.

Remember, though, that no two people are exactly alike in what they seek: one child's punishment may be another's reward. So be alert for individual differences.[11]

In providing punishment for misbehavior, be aware that the child's actions may be a ploy to get attention or to gain status. An unknowing adult may well fall for a child's unconscious scheme, and *reinforce* the undesired behavior. Although you intend to punish a child, the fact that the child gets *attention* or gets you into a struggle for power may give the child the very reward desired—the child *wins* by getting you into the struggle. Consequently, social separation and isolation handled by an adult in a calm manner often is a good strategy for punishment.[12]

Rules

Here are some basic guidelines to use in developing and using rules whether for home or for church.

1. Provide structure and security by establishing reasonable and clear rules appropriate for the child's age and ability.
2. Make rules short and state positively if possible.
3. Be clear about the consequences if rules are not followed.
4. Ask children to help make up some of the rules.
5. Where rules are not necessary, give specific boundaries within which the child must function.
6. As age and dependability increase, broaden the boundaries and renegotiate the rules, involving the child in making decisions.
7. Be firm, consistent, and fair in the application of rules.

Childhood Stress

Of immediate concern to counselors is what child psychologists now are identifying as childhood stress. This condition, they suggest, ultimately affects one's perspective and emotional/physical well-being as an adult.

David Elkind, author of *The Hurried Child,* says that the children of the previous generation can be characterized as those with too little discipline, but those of this decade are the *hurried* children. They are forced to achieve more, earlier, than any other generation. The result of this pressure to achieve, to succeed, to please is a disease in which "children are stressed by the fear of failure—of not achieving fast enough or high enough."[13]

Whereas major emphases in childhood used to be on recreation in a general sense (such as swimming, hiking, pick-up ball games, and make-believe adventures), the focus now is on *specialized* training (such as foreign languages, travel, tennis, soccer, dance, and computers). The most popular of these current activities seem to be those that specialize in competition, where there is a strong desire to teach the finer points, participate in rigorous skill development, and perform in the likeness of adults.

This push in our society also allows children to become status symbols for their parents, teachers, and others who coach them. For example, the push and pride often associated in the past with colleges and prep schools now extends down to private preschools, kindergartens, and special elementary school programs. In all of this is the pressure to get children on the right track early.[14]

Where do you see this in your community? Look for a push on intellectual attainment, such as a gifted and talented program, maybe even down to the kindergarten level. What about the push for physical achievement? Is the level of competition and intensive coaching extending down to the preschool years? How are the children dressing? Are they picking up on designer clothes and styled hair?

Elkind points out that up to about age eight this pressure can be perceived by the child as rejection. After that, they seem to welcome the rapid advance toward adult-oriented achievement. The result is *selective* maturity in the child, with a disjointed sense of wholeness (both as they see it and as we see it). We can mistake this rapid advance in one or two areas as real maturity rather than seeing it simply as a game we and they are playing.[15]

The cure must come from parents, from teachers, from society. Without a change, the qualities that come from five or six years of being a child—playfulness, creativity, adventure, learning to be independent—can be lost in a pressure-packed life that focuses always on bigger and better. In Elkind's words, "It is children's right to be children, to enjoy the pleasures, and to suffer the pains. . . ."[16]

Children and Crisis

Despite the pressures of growing up, this period is perhaps the least stressful in all of life. The child is mobile, has a degree of independence, is adventuresome, greatly resilient, is at the healthiest point in life, and thinks there is an answer and an easy fix-it for everything.

Crises such as divorce, family move, death of a loved one, and major illness do cause disruption, but usually there is great capacity for accepting and moving on with the realities of life. Whereas many adults will be very slow to deal with the stress of acceptance and reintegration involved in resolving crisis situations, children usually will express themselves openly, and very quickly begin to reconstruct their world in light of new situations.

Adults often struggle to look at all the reasons and to explain what should or should not happen; they review many alternatives and search for more; they many times become overwhelmed, and consequently depressed due to the hopelessness they perceive. Children, however, deal with crisis situations much more *concretely;* even their *what if?* questions usually deal with practical matters (like, "What if grandpa doesn't get well; who will take me fishing?").

Children in crisis usually are not ministered to alone; rather, they are cared for as part of a family grouping. This point is important since caregiving in such situations is often directed toward the adults or the family group. Rarely does a child receive his or her share of *needed, individual attention.* Perhaps simply calling this to your attention will be encouragement enough to focus more attention directly on the child.

What should be done? The child needs to tell his or her story without being judged. There is need for emotional and perhaps even physical contact that will be accepting and supportive. Simple statements, reflecting the child's expressions, may help to convey understanding and acceptance: you miss grandpa; you loved him very much; he loved you very much; it is hard to believe that he is no longer with us. Responding with short, simple expressions and, if requested, facts given simply and honestly, will reassure the child. Accompanied by an affectionate hug and a loving look, the child will be able to face the situation with an added sense of personal worth and security.[17]

Fear and anxiety are a normal part of crisis, and usually are short-term. However, if these appear excessive or continue to be expressed after the crisis has been resolved, referral of the parents and child to a specialist is advisable.

Concerning a child's terminal illness, the same principles described above apply. Again, care must be provided in the context of the family system. Many times you will find that the child will be more accepting of the situation than will the parents.

Suggestions to Share with Parents

Here are some rather pointed suggestions that can be shared with parents or adapted for a minister's relations with children in the congregation.

Remember, the phases of childhood development described in this chapter, while occurring about the ages given, are not a rule. There are wide differences among children, even in the same family. Be aware that you can help and encourage, but that you cannot do development *for* a child. With that caution, here are some ideas to share with parents.

1. Be alert to special interests and expressions from your children and seek to cultivate these whenever possible. But be careful not to impose *parental ambitions* on your children; they must develop what God has given *them.*

2. Listen, observe, and talk with children about their schoolwork and home activities. Watch for persistent problems such as the reversing of letters like *saw* and *was.* Discuss your observations with school and church teachers to see if you need to seek consultation with a physician or education specialist.

3. A child's self-esteem is very important. Don't berate when one child is not progressing as fast as another. Encourage and love each child at the level he or she is operating. So much of a child's development happens at a point of *readiness;* be patient.

4. Avoid using adult logic and abstract concepts to explain why a child

should or should not do something. A firm *yes* or *no* or an explicit request often is the best response. ("Because I said so!" may well be a good response for younger children.)

5. *Read* and *write* with your children. Go to the library with them. Read to younger children; then let them tell you the story while pointing to the pictures. Listen to older children read; talk about their response. Encourage creative writing and the writing of letters. Younger children can dictate as you write. Tell short stories to each other.

6. Encourage memory work and reward significant achievement with a homemade certificate or a special surprise. Be patient and listen to all of the rote material; assist when possible.

7. Discuss life experiences together. Talk about programs and commercials you see on television, stories you read together, things that happen at church and in the community. Talk about how you feel about Jesus, church, friends, and your home. Focus on feelings and things you and the child do.

8. Be selective in television viewing. Don't let it be the major influence in your child's home environment.

9. Evaluate the influences in your home. Take a tour. Look at the pictures, the reading material, the arrangement of furniture, the games. Then consider the influence that parents, older brothers and sisters, and neighbors have. Determine the specific things you want to do to influence and nurture your child's development.

Suggestions for Church Ministers

Here are some ideas to assist you in developing a caring and supportive relationship with the children, their parents, and volunteer leaders who work with the children.

Whether you are a minister serving on a large church staff or the pastor of a single-staff church, these ideas can be adapted for your particular situation and ministry style. The only difference should be the frequency with which you do some of the following, not the *quality* of the contact you have with the children or their parents.

Read these over, perhaps adding some ideas of your own; then consider ways to enrich your ministry with children.

1. Make it known that you are a minister to children as well as to adults. Communicate this through the regular channels for church

public relations as well as through your personal contact with children and parents. This doesn't have to be a publicity campaign; rather, it should be an intentional effort to speak to the needs of children with the same frequency that you speak to the needs of adults or of youth.

2. Get acquainted with children as persons in their own right. For example, call them by their names, visit them in their Sunday School departments, occasionally attend one of their socials, or have children visit your home for a party.

3. Look at children as you would an adult. Be aware of your posture when speaking with them. When you are visiting with them individually or in small groups, try to get on eye level.

4. When communicating, use simple, direct language—no big words. Don't ask thought questions like you might use with adults; rather, ask factual questions based on either the material being studied or on what you could expect a child to have experienced. Tell about things that can be seen, felt, or heard.

5. Give some of your teaching time to this age group. This can be done periodically through a children's sermon, in a Sunday School class or a Church Training group, in Vacation Bible School, or through an inquirer's class for children considering a profession of faith.

6. Schedule a regular time to visit the children's departments in your church. Work with department leaders to find a convenient time. On some occasions you could teach or talk with the children about a prearranged topic. At other times perhaps you could be a helper and work at a table with the regular teacher and children.

7. Set up a visitation plan that will assure at least two personal, noncrisis visits *to each child* during ages 6-12. These pastoral calls would be *to visit the child* so that you can get acquainted, learn names, and develop/improve your relationship with each other. One of the best plans is to visit each child as he or she turns eight years old (they will have a desire to know you and will be intrigued by your work by this age). You might plan another visit as each child turns eleven. Each time you visit, be sensitive to the child's understanding of and readiness to consider steps toward a profession of faith.

8. In your formal responsibilities, such as in a worship service, draw

from the world of the child for some of your illustrations, refer occasionally to some of the lessons and songs children are using in Sunday School, and periodically ask all ages to participate in an activity that children love and can do well. If you feel comfortable doing it, use a child from time to time in place of an adult to perform a congregational activity like reading Scripture, praying, or giving a report at business meeting.

9. Conduct a periodic conference for parents. The emphasis might change from time to time, but the general focus should be on family life, parenting, and religious education of children. Conduct some of these sessions yourself, and invite specialists in for others. Ask parents to help identify topics to be considered. Many churches are able to include these sessions during their regular training periods, using materials produced by denominational offices.

10. Provide crisis care for children just as you do for adults. They rejoice, and they sorrow—just in a more concrete way than do older persons. They experience pressure, and they get depressed —but their high activity level usually helps them snap back faster than adults. When counseling with them, ask them to *name* their feelings, or to tell you what the feelings look like. Be accepting; empathize with the child. Try to give assurance that he or she is loved and cared for. When praying, suggest that the child talk with God. If the child is hesitant, ask if you should take turns praying or if he or she would rather have you pray.

11. To help with faith development, tell and retell the great stories of the Bible and of the church. Talk with children about the stories, and encourage them to tell the ones they like to hear.

12. Involve children in the mission and witness of the church in the community. Whenever possible, let children participate in acts of Christian service and outreach along with older church members.

13. Provide opportunity for cross-generation learning and fellowship. Engage all ages on a regular basis in some meaningful activity. This is referred to in a number of ways, like extended family, intergenerational education, family clusters, and all-age learning. The idea is to break down barriers among the age groups.

14. Children tend to mark their religious growth by significant events. Determine the regular events (such as Easter, baptism,

and homecoming) that are important to your congregation, and the personal events (such as birth of a brother or sister, moving, and starting back to school) that are important to children. Develop consistent ways to recognize and/or celebrate such occasions. These become the rituals to which children refer as they build their religious concepts in later years.

15. Be aware that the church is teaching its young through every activity, whether planned or unplanned. The structured teaching is but a small part; the influence of shared life is a major part. Examine with a critical eye the life and ministry of your church. The style of Christian living, the level of caring, and the quality of life together will be the overwhelming determinants on the religious convictions developed by those growing up in your congregation.

Notes

1. The equipping role of the minister in assisting parents is an increasing concern in our society. See, for example, George Gallup, Jr., and David Poling, *The Search for America's Faith* (Nashville: Abingdon, 1980), pp. 41-55.

2. The subject of faith development is crucial for Christians; it is at the root of our reason for being. To acquaint yourself more thoroughly with what is happening to persons and ways to be more effective in assisting them—*and in nurturing your own faith development*—see Bruce P. Powers, *Growing Faith* (Nashville: Broadman Press, 1982).

3. See Robert J. Havighurst, *Developmental Tasks and Education*, Third Ed. (New York: David McKay Co., 1972), pp. 19-35.

4. Adapted from Robert J. Havighurst, *Developmental Tasks and Education*, 3rd ed. (New York: David McKay Co., 1972), pp. 19-35.

5. Rudolf Dreikus and Loren Grey, *A Parents' Guide to Child Discipline* (New York: Hawthorne Books, 1970), pp. 12 ff.

6. Ibid., p. 14.

7. Ibid.

8. Ibid.

9. Ibid., p. 15.

10. An excellent resource on the systemic nature of pastoral care is E. Mansell Pattison, *Pastor and Parish—A Systems Approach* (Philadelphia: Fortress Press, 1977).

11. Dreikus and Grey, p. 21.

12. Ibid., p. 17.

13. David Elkind, *The Hurried Child* (Reading: Addison-Wesley, 1981), p. xii.

14. Ibid., p. 36 f.

15. Ibid., p. 189.

16. Ibid., p. 200.

17. Haim G. Ginott, *Between Parent and Child* (New York: The Macmillan Company, 1965), pp. 145-46.

Additional Bibliography

Cully, Iris V. *Christian Child Development.* San Francisco: Harper and Row, 1979.

Davis, Cos H., Jr. *Children and the Christian Faith.* Nashville: Broadman Press, 1979.

Dreikus, Rudolf, and Loren Grey. *A Parents' Guide to Child Discipline.* New York: Hawthorne Books, 1970.

Duvall, Evelyn Millis. *Evelyn Duvall's Handbook for Parents.* Nashville: Broadman Press, 1974.

Eimers, Robert, and Robert Aitchison. *Effective Parents, Responsible Children.* New York: McGraw-Hill, 1977.

3
Adolescence: Stuck in the Middle
James L. Minton

Any effort to define adolescence precipitates several questions. Do you define adolescence based on when it starts? Do you define adolescence based on what is going on during that period? Do you define adolescence based on what happens as you emerge from adolescence into early adulthood? All three of these questions are valid in developing a definition.

Relative to when adolescence begins, many suggestions have been offered:

- When the levels of adult hormones rise sharply in the bloodstream.
- When they first think about dating.
- When girls are 10 years old; when boys are 12.
- When an interest in the opposite sex begins.
- When they become unexpectedly moody.
- When children turn 13.
- When they form exclusive social cliques.
- When they think about being independent of their parents.
- When they worry about the way their bodies look.
- When they enter seventh grade.
- When their friend's opinions influence them more than what their parents think.
- When they begin to wonder who they really are.[1] There is a kernel of truth in each of these statements, yet none can stand alone as a definition of the beginning of adolescence.

Relative to what is going on during the adolescent period, just use your imagination for a definition. Youth of the eighties are bombarded from every direction by "environmental forces" that bend, stretch, and distort their senses of reality and worth. Two key words emerge for the adolescent: status and survival.

What happens as the young person passes out of adolescence into young adulthood may be more clearly defined. No chronological age can be affixed, but several things become evident according to Robert J. Havighurst:

• Selected and prepared for an occupation.
• Developed intellectual skills and concepts necessary for civic competence.
• Achieved socially responsible behavior.
• Prepared for marriage and family life.
• Developed a value system as a guide to ethical behavior.[2]

Definitions

With this material as background, we now will look at three different perspectives from which to view adolescence as we develop definitions for each perspective. The different perspectives may be stated simply as biological, social, and psychological.

Social scientists with a "biological" orientation might define adolescence as that time between the onset of puberty and the completion of bone growth. Social scientists with a "psychological" orientation might define adolescence in terms of how adolescents think and feel about themselves and their world. Theorists with a "social" orientation (psychologists or sociologists) might define adolescence in terms of the part adolescents play in the larger society—neither a child nor an adult, but someone in-between.

Biologically, adolescent behavior is explained in terms of the physical changes undergone by adolescents. Psychologically, adolescent behavior is explained in terms of changes in thinking and feeling (personality development). Socially, adolescent behavior is explained as a response to a marginal status in society. Any attempt at a complete definition of adolescence would have to include each of these.

Theories

Let us now move into the theories of adolescent development. These theories are generally placed into four categories: biological, sociological, psychoanalytical, and cognitive.

Biological Theroists: *G. Stanley Hall and Arnold Gesell*

The first of the major biological theories of adolescence was formulated by G. Stanley Hall (1904, 1905). Hall was heavily influenced
by the work of Charles Darwin and sought to apply the principles of
evolution to an understanding of adolescent development.[3] Hall's con-
tention was that in the course of their development, children would
progress through a series of stages similar to those through which the
race had progressed in its evolutionary history. Hall's "recapitulation
theory" also suggested that the course of development was largely
genetically predetermined. Therefore, he strongly urged parents not to
be too upset with the way their off-spring were acting in any particular
stage because it would pass, just as our history did. Hall advocated that
it would come and go regardless of the child's environment because the
course of development was determined by genetics alone.

Subsequent evidence of anthropological nature (not including obvious Christian beliefs)—demonstrating that children do indeed behave
very differently in different cultures, and demonstrating as well that the
environment does have a significant effect on a child's development—
has largely invalidated this aspect of the theory.[4]

One aspect of Hall's theory has found limited contemporary support.
He described adolescence as a time of "storm and stress." This was an
expression borrowed from a literary movement of the time, and Hall
thought that adolescence paralleled the movement's commitment to
excessive idealism and rebelliousness against established order among
other things. Most theories will agree that there are stormy and stressful
times in adolescence. Some will go even further and suggest that these
times are necessary and are the motivating force in developing a stable
self-concept.

A second major biological theorist was Arnold Gesell. Like Hall,
Gesell based his developmental theories on the belief that biological
factors were largely responsible for the personality characteristics of
children at various stages in their development. Unlike Hall, however,
he gave the environment an important role in accounting for variations
among individuals.[5]

Gesell's theory has been described as a maturational theory, a spiral
growth theory, and an age profile theory. His theory is called a maturational theory because of his strong belief that various capabilities as well

as personality characteristics result from the genetically determined unfolding of a maturational sequence. It is called a spiral growth theory because it involves the individual making progress, followed by a regression, followed by even further progress. This regression or "fall back" time gives the individual time to consolidate the gains made in progression and better assimilate them. And finally, it is an age profile theory because much of Gesell's work described the progress made by the adolescent at different age levels.

Gesell's age levels for adolescence began at 10 and ended at 16. He was ahead of his time to start at 10 years old, but he stopped several years short at 16. Gesell was aware of the weaknesses in such an approach as this, but he did provide a measuring stick for accomplishments and characteristics for the young person based on a chronological age.

Here is a short summary of Gesell's age levels.

• *Ten-Year-Old.* Is well adjusted, highly sensitive to fairness, confident, obedient, and fond of home. Is careless in appearance and not interested in the opposite sex.

• *Eleven-Year-Old.* Is moody, restless, rebellious, and quarrelsome. Is given to long periods of silence and argues with both parents and siblings.

• *Twelve-Year-Old.* Much of the turbulence of the eleven-year-old has disappeared. Becomes more reasonable and tolerant. Is more influenced by his peers, more independent of his parents, and becomes painfully aware of his appearance. Is for the first time showing interest in the opposite sex.

• *Thirteen-Year-Old.* Is sullen, withdrawn, and very sensitive to criticism. Is tense, critical, and highly self-conscious. Has fewer friends than a year ago, but the ones he does have are a lot closer.

• *Fourteen-Year-Old.* Is suddenly an extrovert. He is confident and outgoing. Spends hours discussing personalities and characters with his friends and has frequent identifications with heroes.

• *Fifteen-Year-Old.* Has a rising spirit of independence. Is boisterous, rebellious, and unpredictable. Has increased tensions. Conflicts with parents and school personnel are on the rise. It doesn't seem like it, but fifteen is the beginning of self-control.

• *Sixteen-Year-Old.* Is self-confident and has a more balanced and integrated personality. He is cheerful, friendly, outgoing, well-adjusted, and shows very little rebelliousness. Is future oriented and the prototype of the preadult.[6]

Gesell's theory has several weak points. Girls are usually 1½ to 2 years ahead of boys in terms of biological changes at the beginning of adolescence. Chronological age is not the best index of social, emotional, and physical development during adolescence. And finally, these profiles don't take into consideration early and late maturers or the various affects of home, school, or peer groups.

Sociological Theorists: *Robert J. Havighurst*

Havighurst is possibly the best-known sociological theorist regarding adolescent development. In the early fifties, he identified ten developmental tasks for the adolescent. The young person strives to accomplish these tasks as he progresses through the adolescent period. After twenty years, Havighurst revised his work and presented a set of eight tasks. These tasks represent the skills, knowledge, functions, and attitudes that young people have to acquire through physical maturation, social expectations, and personal effort. Mastery of adolescent tasks results in maturity. Failure to master the adolescent tasks results in anxiety, social disapproval, and quite probably the inability to function as a mature person. A brief description of each of the eight tasks follows. The reader must be reminded that there are significant differences in developmental tasks in the upper, middle, and lower classes in the United States.[7]

• Forming new and more mature relationships with agemates of both sexes. The adolescent must move from the same-sex interests and playmates of middle childhood to establish heterosexual friendships. This task is the forerunner of normal adult relationships.

• Achieving a masculine or feminine social role. Certain behaviors, attitudes, and values are expected of men and women. Social forces are causing changes in what is expected of a man and what is expected of a woman. Unless adolescents accept their own sexuality as a male or female and find an acceptable sex role, they will feel and be maladjusted.

• Accepting one's physique and using the body effectively. Adolescents are often extreme in their concern over the physical developments of their own bodies. Some changes are happening too fast while others are going too slow. Some adolescents are pleased with their bodies, but most can easily find faults. Most adolescents wonder if they are "normal."

• Achieving emotional independence from parents and other adults. Up to this point, children have depended on parents for love, praise, and tenderness. Now they must develop understanding and respect for their parents without the emotional dependence. Peer interaction facilitates this growth, but it is a slow process and need not be an abrupt happening.

• Selecting and preparing for an occupation. One of the main goals for the adolescent is to decide what to do with his or her life vocationally and then get ready to do it. This task is becoming increasingly more difficult as our economy changes and industry progresses to its present level of automation.

• Preparing for marriage and family life. Patterns of marriage and family living today are being readjusted to the changing economic, social, and religious characteristics of society. Educational demands put off marriage for some while it encourages marriage in others. Living together and trial marriages have developed to challenge traditional concepts.

• Desiring and achieving socially responsible behavior. Sweeping changes in life-styles, especially in the area of marriage and family life, have clouded this task for the adolescent. Society now provides numerous models of apparently "socially acceptable behavior" involving cohabitation, communal living, and other varieties of hetero- and homosexual behavior.

• Acquiring a set of values and an ethical system as a guide to behavior. All through childhood, the individual is educated into the parental value system. As an adolescent, the individual's values are tested outside of the family circle. Then, the adolescent must either accept or reject family teachings, but rejection demands that an alternative must be found. Through this method, the adolescent assembles his personal value system and philosophy of life.

Psychoanalytical Theorists. *Erik Erickson and James Marcia*

Erikson's theory of adolescence drew heavily upon the work of Sigmund Freud but resulted in a much more practical application. Erikson described eight stages of human development. In each stage the individual must confront a conflict area exclusive to the stage. The confrontation produces one of two totally different reactions. One is positive; the other negative. Obviously a negative reaction produces problems and impedes progress to the next stage.

For the adolescent, Erikson labeled the task: identity versus identity confusion. The real effort here is to establish a sense of personal identity since the individual has dealt with identity crises prior to the adolescent years. Erikson feels that during adolescence there must be an integration of all converging identity elements and a resolution of conflict that he divided into seven major parts.[8] The seven parts of the conflict are expressed as bipolar tendencies.

• Temporal perspective versus time confusion. Adolescents must develop a stable concept of time as it relates to their changing self and their eventual position in adult society. They must be able to coordinate the past and the future so they can understand how long it takes to find their own sense of life plans.

• Self-certainty versus self-conciousness. Adolescents must develop self-confidence based on experiences so they can believe in themselves and feel that they have a reasonable chance to accomplish future aims. Self-image and social relationships play important roles in the accomplishment of this task.

• Role experimentation versus role fixation. In the attempt to discover who he or she is, the adolescent discovers many things that he is not. He can experiment with many different identities, personalities, ideas, philosophies, ways of walking and talking. Identity emerges because of this experimentation. The goal is to reject the negative roles experimented with and adopt the most positive role possible.

• Apprenticeship versus work paralysis. The goal of this task is to lead the adolescent toward focusing on productive involvement in a vocation and rejecting inactivity. The adolescent must begin to experiment or entertain ideas of possible avenues of life works.

• Sexual identity versus bisexual confusion. Resolving the sexual identity crises involves identifying with an appropriate sex role and rejecting bisexual tendencies. Developing a clear identification with one sex or the other is an important basis for future heterosexual intimacy and as a basis for a firm identity.

• Leadership polarization versus authority diffusion. Adolescents must become aware of their leadership potential or their lack of it. There are times when the adolescent must lead, and there are times where he must be led. Willingness to be open to whichever situation exists for the young person is important.

• Idealogical commitment versus confusion of ideals. This conflict is closely related to all of the others because a value system, or lack of it, conditions how the adolescent deals with the other six areas of conflict. As our society becomes more lax in its standards, it becomes increasingly harder for young people to get a clear picture of ideals and make commitments.

Many studies have followed Erikson's in attempting to deal with the identity of adolescents. James Marcia provides a very useful description of adolescent identity employing the words *crisis* and *commitment*. Not to be considered in their normal context, these words have an expanded meaning as we look at adolescent identity. The word *crisis* is understood to mean any conflict encountered by the adolescent with respect to identity. *Commitment* is understood to mean any resolving of the previously mentioned types of crisis. Within this framework, it is possible to develop four areas of identity status. These are numbered because they are, within limits, sequential.

1. *Identity confusion.*—The adolescent in this state has not had any identity crisis and has made no commitment. No crisis/no commitment. They have not thought seriously about a possible occupation and are not too concerned about it. They seem to be uninterested in ideological matters or feel one view is as good as the other. "Withdrawal" seems to be the best word to characterize this stage.

2. *Identity foreclosure.*—The adolescent in this state is committed but has not experienced a crisis. No crisis/commitment. The most common examples of foreclosure involve individuals whose political, religious, and vocational decisions have essentially been made for them by their parents, or sometimes by their peers. They become what others intend them to become, without really deciding for themselves. Their security lies in avoiding change or stress.

3. *Identity moratorium.*—The adolescent in this state has experienced crisis but has made no commitment. Crisis/no commitment. A time of moratorium is extremely important for the adolescent. As defined by Erikson it is that period when the adolescent is clearly neither a child nor an adult. This stage is the time for the adolescent to question what types of commitments he will make when faced with the multitude of crises that he will experience.

4. *Identity achievement.*—The adolescent in this state has experienced different crises and has made various commitments. Crisis/commitment. He has a stable self-definition, has committed to a course of preparation or has prepared for a vocation, and understands his opportunities and limitations.

In summary, in the first instance, the adolescent does not know who he or she is, and does not care (identity confusion); in the second, identity has been imposed on the adolescent either by parents or sometimes by the state (foreclosure); in the third, the adolescent is trying to discover who he or she can and will be (moratorium); in the last instance, the adolescent has achieved an identity (identity achieved).[9]

Cognitive Theorist: *Jean Piaget and David Elkind*

Piaget was probably the best known and by far the most influential of all cognitive theorists. He divided the individual's stages of cognitive development into four major parts. Sensorimotor and preoperational stages generally cover from birth through seven years of age. The adolescent years come into focus during the later half of the third stage (concrete operational) and all of the fourth stage (formal operational). The concrete operational stage has an age range of eleven years old to fourteen or fifteen years old and deals with propositional thinking and the ability to deal with the hypothetical. Piaget was quick to point out that these ages were only an approximation. In fact, some recent testing of college freshmen revealed that only about half of them had reached formal operational thinking.

David Elkind, a prominent Piagetian psychologist, brought into focus the concept of adolescent egocentrism. Elkind proposed that egocentrism may be a "bridge between the study of cognitive structure on the one hand and the exploration of personality dynamics" on the other.

The adolescent must learn to distinguish between other people's thoughts and his own. Because the adolescent is so preoccupied with his own behavior, he believes that others are, also. This egocentrism leads to two characteristics of adolescent behavior: the construction of an "imaginary audience" and the creation of a "personal fable." The imaginary audience influence causes the adolescent to feel like he is on "stage" or constantly being watched. Because he makes up this audience, the audience knows everything he knows—all of his personal shorcomings and problems. The personal fable influence can cause the adolescent to feel that his experience is totally unique and that no one has ever been this good or this bad off.

The imaginary audience gradually gives way to the real audience, and the personal fable gives way to a deeper understanding of reality. And with a greater grasp of reality, adolescent egocentrism fades and adulthood begins to emerge.

Theories in Practice: Ministry Issues

The first part of this chapter has been an attempt to deal very *briefly* with some *lengthy* theories as a means of introducing the reader to the different views of adolescent development. The rest of this chapter will deal with practical applications and considerations of the previously mentioned theories.

The adolescent functions in a variety of "worlds," including school, home, the peer group, and hopefully the church. In many cases, the adolescent is a somewhat different person in each world. As a result of this, a school teacher might think he is beyond hope. Adding to the confusion in all of this is the application of Gesell's "spiral growth theory" which has a roller coaster affect on the behavior and attitude of the adolescent. In Gesell's theory, all the even years were peaceful while the odd-numbered years were turbulent. Thus a good year was followed by a bad year. This might help explain to that Sunday School teacher in the ninth and tenth grade department why the tenth-graders just promoted seem like different people than they were as ninth-graders last year.

It must be noted that it rarely falls so neatly into a package of one year; however, the sequence of good-bad does seem to hold true. It is very rare for an adolescent to string together two full "good" years. For some adolescents the years become a matter of months. A rough thirteenth year may be over in six months. Obviously, a lot of environmental factors come into play at this point. All of the "worlds" at this time are within the sphere of influence. Maybe the best advice to parents or youth workers during this time would be to be a little more tolerant and understanding of the "bad" years and a little more appreciative and encouraging during the good years.

It is not totally unheard of for an adolescent to experience very little of the up-down, good-bad syndrome, but it is very unusual. When it does happen like that, some research has indicated that later in life the adolescent, now an adult, experiences the roller coaster effect and it happens at a time that is not nearly as acceptable as it would have been during adolescent years.

Of major concern during development is the adolescent's search for identity and a strengthening of his self-image. Merton Strommen, in his book *Five Cries of Youth,* said that almost three fourths of all young people are struggling with a low self-regard at one time or another.

A good, positive self-image is a must for an adolescent and it might well be the hardest thing for the adolescent to achieve. As young people function in the world, they watch television, go to movies, read magazines, and they see other young people and young adults. But the others they see are models and movie stars, and they don't look like that. So because they don't look or act like the models and movie stars, something must be wrong with them. They are not alright because they don't measure up. Also, life doesn't go as smoothly as in the movies or on television, so something must be wrong with the adolescent. Adolescents might or might not understand with their heads that it's "make believe," but they rarely understand with their hearts that what they see is not real.

Physical appearance and beauty are not at their peek for the adolescent during junior high or early senior high. They do not look as good as the young stars they see on screen and tube. The fact that they have skin, hair, teeth, voice, and weight trouble does not contribute to helping the self-image situation either. The adolescent is undergoing a tremendous amount of physiological changes, many of which affect outward appearance. Either too much or too little of anything appearance-wise at this time can be devastating. The key words here for the adolescent seem to be *normal* and *average,* both of which they are not.

Another situation that does not help self-image at all is the fact that the adolescent thinks that the internal struggles that he is going through are reflected on the outside. In other words, because he looks bad on the inside to himself, he thinks he looks bad on the outside to others.

In dealing with problems of self-image, the mandate is twofold: help the adolescent know and understand that he is not a finished product and go to great lengths to avoid calling attention to his appearance. Do not get caught up in the popular pastime among young people of putting each other down. It's acceptable for them to put each other down but not for an adult to do it. The put-down is one of the all-time classic defense mechanisms because if you make somebody else look bad it helps you look just a little bit better. But it should be taboo for the adult.

With regard to the finished product, remind young people that the youth years are like practice for the big game—life. It's OK to make mistakes and mess up in practice—that's what it's for. The important thing is the game—life. However, because the adolescent lives in the "now," care should be taken not to dwell too much on the future or the fact that it's going to get better. The young person wants help for right now—today!

Developing a value system is of prime importance to the adolescent because these will be the guidelines for living and functioning in the world. Parents, minister, and other Christian adults make contributions and influence this sytem but so does the peer group. The family has, for most young people up to this point, been of primary importance. However, as the adolescent years emerge, the family moves from primary status to secondary status, and the peer group moves into the primary slot. What the peer group thinks and does becomes a major influence. Parents especially should be aware of this and not resent it but should also be concerned about the company their young people keep. Parents should be encouraged to meet and get to know friends and families of friends.

A value system and identity are closely linked, and during this time a real dilemma for parents and even ministers comes into focus. As an adolescent seeks to develop his identity, according to Marcia, he moves through the stages of confusion, foreclosure, and moratorium on the way to achievement. Foreclosure, as previously mentioned, is an almost automatic adoption of parental values and commitments. Then the move into moratorium is a time to question and evaluate and reevaluate and have a time where there are no real commitments. The young person must have this time of searching in order to progress to the achieved identity stage. The true dilemma for the parents and those who would minister to the young person surfaces at this point. These questions have to be considered: Do you really allow your young person to experience moratorium or do you try to prevent it? Do you allow moratorium but ignore it? Do you allow moratorium in all areas but religious development?

The only concrete answer to the previous questions is that it is virtually impossible to prevent moratorium. All young people will experience moratorium in some form or the other. There will also be varying degrees of involvement in moratorium. Some adolescents pass through it only slightly inconvenienced while others are almost devastated by it.

Ministers and Christian parents want to say that there are certain truths and certain standards that we uphold and adhere to and so must our adolescents. The adolescents on the other hand are saying that maybe they need to see for themselves and experience some things before they accept them. Maybe they will adopt the same beliefs, but they want to base their acceptance on their own involvement and experiences rather than someone else's.

Perhaps the best help in being able to deal with moratorium is to be aware that it is happening. It is easier said than done, but perhaps parents, if they are aware of what is taking place, could temper their reactions to problem situations so as not to raise a wall but keep the lines of communication open. As long as parents and young people and ministers and young people are talking, problems can be dealt with. When there is no talking, nothing is accomplished.

In the area of relationships with parents and other adults, it is helpful to consider the fact that middle-aged adult personality and adolescent personality are very different. While not all adults and not all adolescents fall into the types described, the following comparisons show distinct differences which can lead to disagreements.[10]

• Adults are cautious, based on experience; the adolescent is daring and willing to try new things but lacks judgment based upon experience.

• Adults are oriented to the past and compare the present with the way things used to be; the adolescent's only reality is the present. The past is irrelevant and the future is dim and uncertain.

• Adults are realistic and sometimes cynical about life and people; the adolescent is idealistic and optimistic.

• Adults are conservative in manners, morals, and mores; the adolescent challenges traditional codes and ethics and experiments with new ideas and life-styles.

• Adults are generally contented, satisfied, and resigned to the status quo; the adolescent is critical, restless, and somewhat unhappy with the way things are.

• Adults want to stay young and sometimes fear age; the adolescent wants to be grown-up but never wants to become old.

The personal fable and the imaginary audience were mentioned earlier in this chapter. Much of the discipline problems with young people, especially in groups, can be attributed to the imaginary audience theory. The adolescent thinks that wherever he goes and whatever he does, all eyes are on him so he covers his true self by acting out. If he shows the world a real tough guy, they may not see a timid guy underneath. If he shows the world the rude, abrasive guy, they may not see the sensitive guy underneath. The first question in most discipline problems is what is trying to be hidden or covered up.

The personal fable has two somewhat different manifestations. On one hand, the adolescent feels that no one else in the world is having the same problems he is having. No one else has a terrible complexion. No one else is too tall for the weight. No one else has a body odor problem. No one else's hair grows in four different directions. On the other hand, the personal fable manifestation gives the young person a sense of invincibility or immortality. Death and sickness can't touch him because he's not like everyone else. These young people are hit really hard when close friends or family members are lost.

Perhaps the best way to deal with the imaginary audience and personal fable is to endure it. As the adolescent matures and begins to develop a stronger sense of reality, both of these areas seem to ease off and cease to be a problem.

Development of the adolescent's sexuality and his interest in the opposite sex are major influences in his daily functioning. Anyone working with young people needs to research dilligently both of these subjects. The tradegy is that if adults wait until adolescence to begin discussing sexuality and sexual development, it is much too late. Middle and upper elementary years are the times to deal with this area.

Interest in the opposite sex will come just a bit later than upper elementary years for girls and a little later than that for boys in most cases. It is generally agreed that girls are one to two years ahead of boys physiologically and socially in many instances. Boys do not seem to catch up until around the age of fourteen or fifteen. This is one reason that coeducational classes at the junior high level of Sunday School presents problems. A seventh grade girl and a seventh grade boy are two different people. The seventh grade boy may just be beginning to think about girls, while the seventh grade girl is already looking at boys. But she is looking at ninth grade boys and not the seventh grade boys her own age. This is obviously an oversimplification, but it emphasizes the point that there is a social and physical gap in the junior high years.

The latter part of this chapter has been a brief attempt to mention some possible problem areas for young people. Anyone working with adolescents might want to use these as springboards to go further into the study of adolescence.

Growing up at any time is tough, but there may never have been as tough a time as right now. The key word for parents, ministers, and anyone else working with adolescents is *survival.* Help your young people survive adolescence in one piece. It can be done with love, care, and understanding. Many survive without that, but they are not in one piece.

It is also tough trying to raise and minister to this age group. It is unfortunate that we cannot see how the Master Teacher spent this time, but we have no biblical account of the adolescent years of our Lord. Too bad—we could have learned a lot.

Notes

1. John S. Dacey, *Adolescents Today* (Glenview, Ill.: Scott, Foresman and Co., 1982), p. 5.

2. Robert J. Havighurst, *Developmental Tasks and Education* (New York: David McKay Co., Inc., 1952), p. 33.

3. Guy R. LeFrancois, *Adolescents* (Belmont, Calif.: Wadsworth Publishing Co., 1981), p. 108.

4. Ibid.

5. Ibid, p. 111.

6. Arnold Gesell, Frances Ilg, and Louise Ames, *Youth: The Years from Ten to Sixteen* (New York: Harper and Row, Publishers, 1956).

7. F. Phillip Rice, *The Adolescent* (Boston: Allyn and Bacon, Inc., 1981), p. 70.

8. Ibid., p. 57.

9. LeFrancois, p. 134.

10. This is an adaptation from W. J. Anderson, *Design for Family Living*

(Minneapolis; T. S. Denison & Co., 1964), and quoted from F. Phillip Rice, *The Adolescent* (Boston: Allyn & Bacon, Inc., 1981).

Additional Bibliography

Adams, Gerald R., and Gullotta, Thomas. *Adolescent Life Experiences.* Monterey, Calif.: Brooks/Cole Publishing Co., 1983.

Forisha-Kovach, Barbara. *The Experience of Adolescence.* Glenview, Ill.: Scott, Foresman and Co., 1983.

Gregory, Thomas West. *Adolescence in Literature.* New York: Longman, 1980.

Haviland, Jeannette M., and Scarborough, Hollis S. *Adolescent Development in Contemporary Society.* New York: D. Van Nostrand Co., 1981.

Hopkins, J. Roy. *Adolescence: The Transitional Years.* New York: Academic Press, Inc., 1983.

Ingersoll, Gary M. *Adolescents.* Lexington, Mass.: D.C. Heath and Co., 1982.

LeFrancois, Guy R. *Adolescents.* Belmont, Calif.: Wadsworth Publishing Co., 1981.

Narramore, Bruce. *Adolescence Is Not an Illness.* Old Tappan, N.J.: Fleming H. Revell Co., 1980.

Santrock, John W. *Adolescence.* Dubuque, Iowa: William C. Brown Co., 1981.

Sprinthall, Norman A., and Collins, W. Andrew. *Adolescent Psychology.* Reading, Mass.: Addison-Wesley Publishing Co., 1983.

Stevens-Long, Judith, and Cobb, Nancy J. *Adolescence and Early Adulthood.* Los Angeles: Mayfield Publishing Co., 1983.

Thornburg, Hershell D. *Development in Adolescence.* Monterey, Calif.: Brooks/ Cole Publishing Co., 1982.

4
Young Adulthood: Starting on Your Own
J. Thom Meigs

Interestingly enough the word *adult* comes from the Latin *adolescere*, which means for one thing "to grow up." The word itself tends to be neutral about the nature of growth. However, it does imply *process* more than the *possession* of a special status or particular faculty or capacity. In this sense, however "ripe" Angela or Chris view their established years of development, they cannot really think of themselves as totally completed persons yet.

The young adult is very much a "wayfarer" or "pilgrim."[1] One personality analyst said that not all adults are indeed adults. Taking one's "givens" in life, a central question becomes, "What do you think your life will be like from now on?" A comic strip character was advised, "There is nothing medical science can do about your condition! I recommend that you have your cartoonist redraw you!" Since that option is ill-advised and a return to the factory is out of order, let us look now at a positive profile and valued "condition" of the young adult.

Characteristics of Young Adulthood

What is it like to be a normal young adult? What happens characteristically during this transitional era? For one thing, Angela and Chris are no longer just dependent *apprentices* on their family, church, and educational systems. What is in order now is their capacity to attain an identity that includes physical maturation, the ability to live intimately with a person of the opposite sex, and hopefully to become well integrated. Chris/Angela have reached a decisive crossroads in their journey.

63

Cruicial Turning Points

Let us look at the word *crisis,* which can mean a "dividing." Young adulthood is a normal time of crisis—whether to move forward and ahead, to go backward to the way it was, or even to stagnate as if one is in a whirlpool of accumulated experiences. A crisis experience is a nonsurprising tension between our aspirations and hopes on the one hand and our finitude/limitedness and vulnerabilities on the other hand. Normal, predictable crises of change and transition both *confront* us with issues of truth, integrity, mercy, and responsibility for actions, and *fortify* us in giving "heart," encouragement, and affirmation. They can be moments of achievement and celebration. They can be tough moments of hard adjustment. Hopefully, as young adults Angela and Chris can utilize effectively their opportunities and teachable moments as well as accept and claim the responsibilities that accompany them.

The young adults' energies, interests, and inspirations have the ability to be directed outward beyond their own individual growth and development. In a sense, they are able to start sailing on their own, for, by and large, Chris has been taught "to navigate and . . . has been provided with charts, albeit they are charts that can be only approximately correct for the currents and reefs change constantly."[2]

One of the tasks that Chris has learned under more or less competent supervision and modeling is how to accept consequences of his decisions, including how the decision is processed, whom he chooses as his confidants to be consulted along the way, and when other persons become involved, such as a pastor or a deacon. Lidz's insight about the young adult may very well be true, "Usually he asks another to share the journey, and soon others join them, bidden and unbidden, and their welfare depends upon his skills and stability."[3]

Camera over there.—Our life development tends to take place in relatively predictable steps or stages. Adaptation to change is a continual facet of life's movement. The film has been rolling. For example, the stage you've left behind has been called "adolescence." Your development up to this point as a "moving into the next layer" of experience includes the ways that you have grown or matured physically and biologically. You're aware of these changes and shapings. The way in which you relate to and view your body is very important. For example, do you sense indeed that your body is a well-intended gift from God to be claimed and taken care of in appropriate goodness and worthwhileness?

Our individual development doesn't take place in a vacuum without other persons. It has a context. Hopefully, it has been a "people making" context. The way in which you have developed has depended on the support and nurture, or the lack of them, received from your family and the quality of inspiration, challenge, and scripting of family, school/education, neighborhood, peers, workplace, government, and religious affiliation. Young adulthood gives a "near to" opportunity to reflect on one's experience and behavior. Part of Christ's tug-of-war is a desire to look ahead or skip ahead while feeling a strong urge to keep his head looking over the shoulder to the past.

Family life and background indeed are something like an "iceberg." Most of us are aware of only a small percentage of what has actually gone on. It does help, however, to discover the feelings, needs, and patterns that were interwoven into our family's fabric. Virginia Satir and others suggest that the family is the "factory" where persons are "made." "You, the adults, are the 'peoplemakers.' "[4]

Family threads.—Chris and Angela need to recognize and to assess something of what their own family was like in order to recognize what differences they want to make or change for themselves. Perhaps it will mean that they will learn to confirm former strengths also. Learning to praise those strengths is a viable and holistic alternative. Much of what they have been encouraged to do is based upon the partial point of departure that begins, "What is wrong with your upbringing?"

Four significant threads of family life surface regardless of the family style. These threads include: self-worth—the concepts and feelings you have about yourself; communication—the ways persons in the system work out the meaning each has for the other; rules—the guidance and structures for how you feel and act; and connection to larger society—the ways and strategies by which the family relates to other people and institutions. These are fairly common working features for most families, whether the family essentially was a troubled or nurturing one.

Troubled families tend to know more about the language of fear and anxiety-riddenness than the language of faith and trust. Self-worth is low or deflated. Communication is indirect, assumptive, circumventing, and sometimes not honest. Rules are very tight, hierarchical, nonnegotiable with a sense of the "everlasting." The connection to society is fearful, blaming, or placating.

Nurturing families on the other hand are interested in the language of faith and trust which includes the developed ability to say to each other, "I am not afraid of you, and there is no need for you to be afraid of me." Self-worth is tenderheartedly firm or high. Communication is clear, nonassumptive, and honest. Rules are certainly necessary, but they show flexibility, appropriateness, ability to change, and human-ness. The connection to society is discerning yet open and hopeful.

Every person then has feelings of worth, either positive or negative. The question that unfolds is, "Which is it for you?" We all communi-cate. The basic question is, "How do we communicate consistently, and what happens as a result of our communication?" We all follow and have rules. "What kind are they, and how well do they work for us?" We are interfaced with society. "How are we linked, and what happens as a result of our style of relatedness?"[5]

Friend or foe?—Young adulthood is a *role of challenge.* Young adults are in a movement toward greater *complexity, competence,* and *integration*[6] as a result of the challenge and support already experienced in their significant settings of life. Complexity here means the total makeup of Angela—thoughts, feelings, values, aspirations, dreams, choices, behaviors, beliefs—in the context of and in interaction with the various systems of her life. As a young friend aptly said, "It's not getting any easier or simpler. And it's a bigger world out there and inside me than I had stopped to imagine."

Some of the basic questions that need to surface are: "What specific and clear developmental issues am I currently tussling with?" "What practical knowledge and life-giving, not life-extracting, skills are called for by these challenges?" "What is available for me in order to gain the skills and working knowledge I need?" It is not just a question of "Who am I now?" It is also *Quo vadis,* "Where do I go from here?"

Levinson's monumental study proposed a term for the young/early adult transition called "the novice phase." This process is more lengthy and complex than at first imagined, beginning at around age 17 and continuing until about 33. Thus, he insists, for instance, that "a young man needs about fifteen years to emerge from adolescence, find his place in adult society and commit himself to a more stable life."[7] The novice phase really has three components or "developmental bridges," each with its own tasks: the early adult transition (roughly ages 17-22), entering the adult world (ages 22-28), and the age thirty transition. Together they serve a singular function: "the process of entry into adulthood." However, the "actual" time or "event-izing" when adult life starts is not set chronologically. In fact, it is a "little bit" elusive. An example of this is the person who may have engaged the vocational choice and chosen a mate sometime in adolescence.

Trying to draw exact chronological boundaries around the age in which young adulthood begins and ends is an uneasy business. Different developmentalists offer varying time frames. As Lucien Coleman suggested, "Trying to define these boundaries with precision is something like attempting to locate a state line on a rural road where there is no marker."[8] In other words, there are no precise visible lines of demarcation. The clues may consist more in the subtle psychological and sociological changes occurring *intra*-personally and *inter*-personally.

Saying good-bye to pre-adult world.—The early adult transition challenges Chris and Angela to say a creative good-bye to the adolescent life structure and to take preliminary, preparatory steps into the adult world. It is a rite of passage for them. It includes how they separate from and yet claim family origin.

Do you remember the way life differed *after* high school from life *during* the high school years? If college is part of the experience, you are on your own in ways that really don't match up to high school. There is a belief that students in college don't "mess around" in the classroom in the ways students often do in high school. One factor in this difference may be the assumption that you're in college because you "want" to be there, not because you "have" to be. Thus, you are expected to manage your behavior both inside and outside the classroom or laboratory in order to accomplish academic goals that you've set.

If you have not gone on to college, you are still expected to learn management of your lives. Whereas the college student is making decisions about such areas as courses and curriculum, non-college persons are making decisions about such things as "full time" work. Nevertheless, as part of the ongoing challenge of the college years is the issue, "What's ahead? Will the future—those days not yet lived or experienced—offer a sense of welcome and a 'come on ahead; you can trust me?' "

A network of influences.—Young adults come out of a network of personal settings. You are in the middle. Coming out of this position are a number of influences: church, family, work, acquaintances, physical exercise, intimate friends, extracurricular activities, and crises.

There are at least four levels of the social world in which your development takes place: (1) immediate personal settings, such as family; (2) the network of personal settings and how these have influenced you; (3) large institutions and organizations; and (4) culture which permeates and influences all levels of these systems.[9]

These systems require balancing acts in terms of the demands placed upon you. One friend shared with me, "I find it difficult to parcel out my time. I find I am constantly forcing myself to decide between being with my friends and getting my work done. My emotional filter system gets clogged up with dust at times." The stress that is experienced is part of the price you pay. Stress has to do both with your expectations and actual experiences. If there is a differential between what the person "expects" to be happening (wants to be occurring) and what one is actually "experiencing," that difference means stress. The demands outweigh or imbalance the resources.

Getting into formation.—In Levinson's "provisional" or "novice" phase, men are especially required to face four basic tasks: (1) forming and living out a "Dream," which is "a vague sense of self-in-adult-world" and the fitting of it into your "life structure," (2) forming mentor or teachable/learning relationships with significant others who can guide, advise, and facilitate the realization of the "Dream," (3) forming an occupation or pursuing a career as a way of life, while enhancing skills and credentials, and (4) developing and forming intimate relationships. This fourth task explores the meaning of love in marriage and family, establishing a basis for affection, emotional disclosure or intimacy, sexuality, respect for authority, friendship, and enduring commitment.[10] None of these above tasks can be finished before the end of this phase. These tasks tend to proceed unevenly, with recurrent ups and downs, and not in a steady way.

Between those ages of 17 and 22 most persons are either building or need to take time to build a framework for "leaving" home and family and to channel a preliminary leap into an "independent" adult world. Although it can be traumatic for some, most persons experience what Levinson calls a "voice within" which speaks to us about "changing" life—building or modifying, excluding or adding, starting or leaving, dismantling or installing, nurturing or combinations of these.

Some of the interesting data supplied by Gail Sheehy in *Passages* defines three basic types of women. The "caregivers" ("nurturants") seek meaning and value from giving to others, and at this time in their 20s are not torn over going beyond or extending the domestic role. The "either/ors" choose either nurturant roles or work/accomplishment roles. The "integrators" ("Super women") are the style who try to combine marriage, career, and motherhood in their 20s.

Morning has broken.—To be or not to be more self-directed is at least part of the question for the young adult. Learning the value of "mutuality" is another part of the question. The value of self-direction emerges in the fact that it is a kind of call to take initiative about one's own life.

Mutuality means the willingness of persons to invest themselves in one another's lives with the purpose of helping to build up each other in care and growth and not to tear down and destroy. In the New Testament, the word *koinonia,* commonly and popularly translated as "fellowship," means in a rooted sense "the equipping of each other for service together in Christ." This is a word that attempts to shorten relational distance and bring persons closer together. Strongly competitive models discourage and disengage you from others. The apostle Paul expressed the substantial difference when he reminded Christians in Philippi that they are partners/partakers in grace and not rivals in spirit. Categories of "winners" and "losers" promote unhealthy tensions of comparison between persons.

Mutuality is a "good news" word. But it will sometimes threaten "the daylights" out of us. Let me illustrate selectively by referring again to Egan and Cowan's interpretation of mutuality.

1. Disclosing and sharing yourself with others in a game-free way when such disclosure is appropriate,
2. Listening to others carefully and trying to understand their point of view . . .
3. Engaging in nondefensive self-exploration when challenged. . . .[11]

The dawning of new mornings and days raises some personal reflections. Examples appear in this manner. "What am I accomplishing, and at what cost?" "What kind of support do I usually look for from other people?" List several adjectives that I believe describe the important dimensions of myself. Name three things I seem to do well. "What is one relationship in my life I would hate to lose?" "What do I think that I will be doing five years from now?"

Never too young to grieve.—An overweight young person was conversing about his tennis game with a friend. "When my opponent hits the ball to me, my brain immediately barks out a command to my body: 'Race up to the net,' it says. 'Slam a blistering drive to the far corner of the court, jump back into the position to return the next volley.' Then my body says, 'Who . . . me?' "

The following sections incorporate a number of characteristics of a normal transitional period that begins with "Who . . . me?" and moves to a more "in-sight-ful" response "Yes . . . this is probably me!"

First, the young adult may at times feel suspended between the past and the future. Girl or woman? Boy or man? Feeling young or old? Some of you will have intense feelings, while others will have very mild feelings about life's movement. Different persons measure its meaning differently.

Second, transitions actualize growing edges, but they are also at times occasions for uprooting, separation anxieties, and particular losses. Indeed, the anxiety of grief is a strong candidate to be elected at these moments. The fact is that we really don't have to vote for its office. Grief as a natural alignment to separation, loss, or even the anticipation/apprehension of separation/loss just tends to show up to make itself known.

Young adults are learning how to understand and to cope with their griefs: exits—entrances; saying good-byes—saying hellos; separation—belonging; giving up—taking on; and adjusting to—reorganizing. Stating that grief is life's unavoidable companion, Ramsay and Noorbergen outline phases and components of grief: shock, disorganization, searching behavior, emotional components (including pining, guilt, anger, shame, protest), letting go, resolution and acceptance, and reintegration.[12] Oates shared a phase called the struggle between fantasy—as if it isn't happening—and reality—knowing that indeed something has changed.[13]

Some losses are inevitable. The point is that we grieve quite naturally over the *loss* of or change over anything/anyone important, crucial, necessary, valuable, or integrally linked to us. Jesus taught, "Blessed are they that mourn, for they shall be comforted" (Matt. 5:4).

Linus of *Peanuts* fame said, "I can't live without that blanket. I can't face life unarmed." There will be "a good many" times when you will wonder why you are "flat," "blah," "down," "depressed," "feeling unarmed" about some of those transitions. As one person explained, "When I graduated from Georgia Tech and got that wonderfully exciting job in Philadelphia, I couldn't understand why I felt so immobilized for a good while." She was born, grew up, and educated all the way through college in Atlanta. That was her place—until now. Depression normally seems to be a "brother or sister" to losses and significant transitions. There will be days in which you would like to buy just a little more time before you really have to face some of these "adult" responsibilities.

A third factor involves quizzing the world, your place in it, your present way of doing things, the order of your values, and relationship to authority figures. "Perhaps I shouldn't be so compliant." "Maybe I need to seek out and find some new friends." "That preacher is so dogmatic." "Prayer?" "I do need to read more." "Why should I vote? I'm only one person." So the tussle goes on between appropriate, healthy self-assurance and the self-made attitude of "I don't need any body. And furthermore what can you do for me?"

Fourth, exploration or experimentation may be an outcropping of one's questioning.[14] "There is no reason why I can't become a little more assertive in pursuing friendship with . . . (members of the opposite sex)." Levinson noted that the neglected parts of oneself tend to rise up to seek expression. Erikson called this a "moratorium," a "time off" or "time out" from "ordinary" role expectations to check out new roles, values, and beliefs. Illustrations of this vary from the high-school student who takes a year or two off to work or enlist in the military, before going on to college, to travel in Europe, or wherever. "I'm going to wait before I join that Sunday School class. I had to go to church all my life—everytime the doors were open."

Out One Era and into Another

Egan summarizes the developmental tasks of moving into and with adulthood: (1) becoming competent, (2) achieving autonomy, (3) developing and implementing values, (4) forming an identity, (5) integrating sexuality into life, (6) making friends and developing intimacy, (7) loving and making a commitment to another person, (8) making initial job or career choices, (9) becoming an active community member and citizen, and (10) learning how to use leisure time.[15]

Vivian McCoy sets out a structure of stages with a different delineation. She calls the first developmental stage, roughly ages 18-22, "Leaving Home." The tasks intertwined to this stage are: (1) breaking/accepting psychological ties, (2) choosing careers, (3) entering work, (4) handling peer relationships, such as whether peers are useful allies in understanding the hold of family, (6) managing time, (7) adjusting to life on one's own, (8) problem solving, and (9) coping with the stress as a companion to change.

The immediate next stage, "Becoming Adult," spans the ages 23-28. The tasks here continue previous ones and also shift to: (1) selecting mate, (2) settling in work and even beginning a career "ladder," (3) parenting and family formation, (4) emerging involvement in community, (5) wise consuming, (6) homeownership, (7) social interactions, (8) achieving autonomy and self-direction, (9) problem solving, and (10) again coping with the stress of change. The "Catch-30" stage, ages 29-34, surfaces further variety: (1) undergirding or searching for personal and meaningful values, (2) reappraising relationships, (3) so-called progress or emergent success in career, (4) accepting and shifting with growing children, (5) roots and sense of permanency of home, (6) problem solving, and (7) handling stress correlated to change.[16]

Themes for Wholesome Living[17]

What Do I Do Well? Most of us would like to carry out our tasks with a nicely put "well, done!" Competence doesn't normally occur as a spectacular Hollywood production. It happens more down to earth without a trumpet of fanfare. Angela and Chris's *sense* of competence is the measurement of confidence they have in their ability to get things done in adequate amounts. Their *actual* competence refers to their ability to carry out these tasks.

At this point let's caringly identify some strengths as well as "soft spots." "Do I indeed see myself as a person who is capable of carrying through and getting things done?" "Do I have the resources needed—'stick-to-it-ness,' inner strength, spiritual reserve—to accomplish goals I have set or dreamed for myself?" "In what areas of life do I especially handle myself well (or even more than adequate)?" What areas would I like to be more effective in than I am?" "Am I willing to express my needs for assistance from others?"

The upsurge of computerization has complicated our perspective. The intrusion of chemical dependency is one of the greatest demonic challenges to the Christian's sense of confidence, as we encounter the world with our sense of mission and creative witness for Christ. As we minister with persons, keep in mind that competence includes such ingredients as the ability to endure reasonable degrees of frustration, subdue egocentrism/narcissism/ "the only me and no one else" impulse, and rightly accept/exercise authority. Set realistic goals that are not beyond your "stretch." Letting others dictate your goals may be a form of unrealistically high goal setting. On the other hand, setting goals that are unusually low or circular may not be beneficial because there is no striving or aspiring involved. An example of this is the young man who majored in physical education in college, not because he liked athletics, but because it happened to be one of the easiest majors.

Self-worth has three important sources: God's creative image in us, conveyed as His children; an inner source, the degree of effectiveness and nourishment of one's own activity; and an external source, the opinions of significant others about oneself. The first two are steadier and more dependable by far than external sources. In fact, the apostle Paul wrote, "Such confidence as this is ours through Christ before God. . . . Our competence comes from God" (2 Cor. 3:4-5, NIV).

In summary, competence refers to "how we do it" in these facets of life: (1) physical/manual abilities, from coordination of body skills to living with handicaps; (2) social/emotional abilities in relating/expecting/reaching out decently, considerately, and faithfully to other persons, how this helps to determine and feeds into feelings of worth, to know what is called for in social situations, and social intelligence— when to respond appropriately; (3) self-management/caring skills; (4) interpersonal skills, including self-presentation, attending and active listening to others, responding to others, and challenging others ethically; and (5) the skills of small-group involvement, which at first seems "so easy."[18] In actual experience it may be more difficult than it appears. "What are the small-group involvements of your life?" "What is the group's goals?" "Does the group encourage helpful or negative conversations?" "Does the group promote competition or diversity within unity?" "What do you do well when you participate in it?"

The ministry of the church can be a facilitator or catalyst for matching persons in groups—Sunday School classes, interest or hobby groups, spiritual nourishment and equipping groups (i.e. prayer and Bible study types), and the Christian identity/discipleship confronting his/ her world.

Young adults want to believe they "belong" and are an integrated part of the community of faith. "This is our church." Jesus gave us a directive for the competency of loving each other (John 15:13-15). Hear some of the Apostle Paul's words as he focuses our confidence "in Christ." "I pray that out of his glorious riches he may *strengthen* you with power through his Spirit in your *inner being,* so that Christ may dwell in your hearts through faith. And I pray that you, being rooted and established in love, may have *power, together with* all the saints . . ." (Eph. 3:16-18, NIV, author's italics). "Then we will *no longer be infants,* tossed back and forth by the waves, and blown here and there by every wind of teaching and by the cunning and craftiness of men in their deceitful scheming. Instead, speaking the truth in love, we will in all things *grow up* into him who is the Head, that is, Christ. From him the whole body joined and held together by every supporting ligament, *grows* and *builds* itself in love, as *each part does its work*" (Eph. 4:14-16, NIV. Study also Eph. 4:22-29 and Phil. 2:4,12-13, author's italics). Therefore, "Each one should test his own actions. . . . Let us not become weary in doing well, for at the proper time we will reap a harvest if we do not give up" (Gal. 6:4,9, NIV).

Can I (We) Make It on MY (Our) Own? Autonomy pertains to our capacity to attain reasonably safe self-sufficiency, but not at the expense of someone else. It is a challenge of moving toward mature, faithful interdependence. Four dimensions interface: (1) our need for approval versus overidentifying and overvaluing another's response, (2) our ability to manage life independently, without continually or grudgingly seeking help from others, (3) the capacity for self-initiated planning, organizing, and problem solving, and (4) awareness of how our needs relate to the needs of others, and thus the ability to integrate or to discern those needs.

"Can I get things done all by myself?" "On a scale 1-10, with 1 representing overly dependent, 10 representing overly independent, where do I find myself?" "Do I seem to be reasonably and fairly interdependent in my work, social life, church life?" "When I need help—whatever its normal form—do I find it easy or awkward to ask for it?"

Autonomous persons are not hermits living isolated on desert islands. They, in fact, recognize their needs for others. They are respectful of the others' needs. Yet, they themselves do not need continuous support, reassurance, and emotional "pats on the back." One young wife struggled with this: "It seems like no matter what I do, I'm watching to see if my husband and others really like it. Sometimes I get so worried about this that I fail to concentrate on what I'm supposed to be doing. I'm beginning to realize how this ties me up. I feel like a puff ball." Be careful of overvaluing the approval of others. "It'll wear your integrity out." Autonomous persons can certainly be married. If one's previous motto was "Do your own thing," then marriage deserves finding and maintaining balance between my/his needs with your/her needs. At one end of the continuum is the one who conveys, "I don't need you at all" and on the other end, "I need you desperately—now—quickly—forever present."

The following open statements are really some exercises to examine dependence, counterdependence, independence, and interdependence. Give one example of an experience in which you have been recently "nongrowthfully" *dependent.* One college student shared, "I regret that I still take all my laundry home for my mom to wash." Share an example of *dependence* enriching to you! A wife wrote, "When I was put to bed to rest because of my anemic condition, my family waited on me. It was a welcomed relief."

Record a "nongrowthfully" *counterdependent* experience. "I can't stand anyone in authority. No one's going to tell me what to do." Then illustrate a growth experience here. "I know I have the ability to write the checks and keep a budget. I refuse to ask his help to untangle my procrastination."

Share an example of a way in which you displayed unproductive *independence.* "I decided to live in an apartment by myself during the fall semester. Boy, am I lonely!" On the other hand, record one beneficial to you. A new Christian in my Sunday School class confessed, "I realized that I don't have to drink at all to have friends." For interdependence, give a nonproductive example, followed by a successful one. "I'm not going to be wishy-washy anymore. We'll talk together about the decisions from now on."

The church's ministry might offer a chance for young adults to review and discuss goals individually, or in forums. Ministry in this sense becomes a "reality presenter." Pay attention to goals that: (1) make sense to you and lead to accomplishments you value, which you are not ashamed of; (2) are concrete rather than blurry and general; (3) are in touch with the resources you have at hand; (4) motivate your willingness to put out; and (5) have a time boundary for completion or renegotiation.[19]

What Do I Believe "In"? What provides you the bases for your ethical and spiritual development? Where do you "pledge your allegiances"? The arena of moral development has attracted the attention of many gifted and yet diverse talents. The self-centered layer, according to these investigators, asks, "Will the results of my behavior be pleasurable or painful for me?" The other-centered layer asks, "Will my behavior show loyalty to my significant affiliations—family, friends, Christ?" The questioning stage asks, "What views of truth, goodness, and so on can I trust?" The relativistic stage asks, "How will my action come out in terms of this overarching standard?" The committed stage asks, "Am I morally clean by the criteria I have chosen?"

Pastoral strategy is interested in these kinds of concerns. "What are the things that are really valuable to me?" "Do I practice my values?" The Scriptures suggest, "Do not neglect your gift. . . . Be diligent in these matters; give yourself wholly to them so that everyone may see your progress. Watch your life and doctrine closely" (1 Tim. 4:14-16, NIV; also 2 Tim. 2:15). In summary it means: "Love the Lord your God with all your heart and with all your soul and with all your mind" (Matt. 22:33, NIV).

Who in This World Am I? The decisive factor of *identity* or *selfhood* for the Christian is our encounter with Christ. "For we are his workmanship, created in Christ Jesus for good works, which God prepared beforehand that we should walk in them" (Eph. 2:10). Identity is also the bridge between oneself and larger society. Out of the numerous possibilities, dreams, and hopes of childhood emerges your pattern/character style. The early childhood question, "Who will I be?" is now taking unique, urgent shape.

For the next few minutes begin with these thought stimulators. "Do

I have a good grasp of who I am and the direction I seem to be going in life?" "Am I ashamed of who I am and what I have done with life, or am I able to smile when all is said and done?" "Am I reasonably satisfied?" "Do I see myself as others see me?" "What/who is the integrating center that gives meaning (the theme) to my life?" "In what social contexts do I feel best about myself?" "In what social contexts do I feel 'smudged into the wallpaper'—a loss of distinctiveness?"

A combination of the theological themes of providence and awareness of the holy allows us to process pastorally where one's ultimate and transcendent meanings of life hold true. "Does the person perceive a divine purpose in his/her life?" "Does he have a sense of basic trust in the world?" "What is sacred to this individual?" "Is he suspicious of divine promises as they have been interpreted to him by a over-promising or rigidly demanding minister?" "Does he believe God intends for him to experience well-being?"[20]

Jesus, in the parallel years of his young adulthood, was faced with the question of authentic and true identity and embraced fully the fact of "this is who I am" to the world. At his baptism John tried to deter him, but Jesus instructed, "Let it be so now, for thus it is fitting for us to fulfill all righteousness." A voice from heaven affirmed, "This is my beloved Son, with whom I am well pleased" (Matt. 4:15,17, RSV). Later, he raised part of the identity question, "Who do people say I am?" "What about you?" "Who do you say I am?" ("Who am I to you?"). Peter answered, "You are the Christ" (Mark 8:27-30, RSV).

New insights are likely to happen if you spend a while completing this: "I am . . ." (or "I am one who . . .") and do this about fifteen times with a different response each time. Then design a presentation of your life mapping, "Let me tell you about where I've come from to get here!" These exercises can be used effectively in caring church groups to develop active listening, acceptance, and understanding of each other's history. The principle of James is a good communication vehicle. "Everyone should be *quick to listen* . . ." (Jas. 1:19).

What Is the Place of Occupation/Work in My Life? "Just a housewife!" "Just a salesman!" Career or occupational choice is a process of decision making. It symbolizes much more than a designed set of skills and functions. It means a way of life. "What do you do?" "Oh, really?" Unfortunately, there are tendencies to form snap judgments about people according to what they "do." Write brief responses to these

open-ended statements: (1) "Choosing a career means for me
_____; (2) I've really considered/dreamed about the following
vocations _____; (3) If I had an ideal career where everything
knitted together 'just right' for me, it would be _____."

"Expanding—narrowing—again expanding—narrowing" is the pattern.[21] The expanding phase broadens the view of options or possibilities. The narrowing movement contracts or squeezes more tightly the focus and eliminates some options in favor of more promising or satisfying ones. "Where does college, postgraduate education fit in?" "Should I go now or wait?" "If we set the wedding for December, will that distract him from his graduate orals?"

A self-inventory might include: "What are my feelings about the way I am preparing myself for a career?" "What are my predominant thoughts and feelings about my present position/work?" "What do I get out of my work?" "What is the workplace environment like?" "What typically goes on there?" "Where am I regarding my 'initial' career choice?"

Pastoral strategy can serve as an enabler for action plans involving goals, resources toward achieving goals, and concrete programs, as well as being a "cheer leader." Vocational guidance, utilizing a variety of persons experienced in particular areas, opens dialogical participation, exploring, and understanding. Christian vocation is more than the work one does, or the career engaged in. It is helping neighbor and being ambassadors for Christ. Has God "called" you? If you are a Christian, the answer is a resounding yes. Learning the *stewardship* of our gifts wherever we work can be a channel of elevating work to a sense of vocation—"calling." "As each has received a gift, employ it for one another, as good stewards of God's varied grace" (1 Pet. 4:10; see 1 Cor. 4:2). In a broad sense, the word *meaning* could be put in the place of "calling." Thus, it might read, "the 'meaning' I give as a Christian to my work is. . . ." "Am I a cheerful participant in the scheme of God's creation?"

The Gift of Sexuality Means to Me . . . ? "Who am I as a God-given sexual being?" Many Christian ethicists suggest that the way in which you see yourself as a sexual being is an important dimension of your overall identity.

This also influences how you relate to others as a sexual person. For example, if you see yourself only as an object of pleasure, then you may be exploited as a sexual pleasure object. Culture through the media, magazines, and advertising especially conveys many double messages and sex-role stereotypes. "What in the world does a bikini-clad beauty have to do with the value and efficiency of that shaving cream, new automobile, or toothpaste?" The beat goes on with that kind of absurdity. Most of us would find a new American car under $2,000 a very good buy, "sexy" or not.[22] What has happened is that commercialism and its myriad of marketplaces has taken away a holistic understanding of a kind of God-intended birthright. Sexuality has been reduced to sex, and sex reduced to the status of a commodity to be dispensed as reward for performance. This reductionism and purely recreational approach also dehumanizes the response-ability to receive, to claim, and to decide about the gift. The "fun sex" mentality is a reflection of a kind of incomplete, distorted valuing. The question pastoral strategy needs to ask again and again is, "Is such sex really honest?"

Assess these sentences carefully. "When I think of myself as a sexual being, I. . . ." (Write a paragraph or two.) "What I learned in my home (from parents) about sexuality was. . . ." "The persons or social settings which introduced me to sexuality were: peers, classes in school, church groups, parents, or. . . ." "What did they teach me and what did I learn about the subject?" Furthermore, shifting gears to a correlated area, "What are several values that are significant to me that relate to my sexual life?" (List these!) "When I envision closeness with a person of the opposite sex, I tend to. . . ." "In terms of my sexuality, marriage for me means. . . ." "What are my expectations about 'women should be' and 'men should be'?" "How do these sex-role expectations affect my behavior?" "A good family life is. . . ." "A good marriage is. . . ."

The church can provide dialogical conversations and forums to deal with society's voices and distortions. Marriage enrichment retreats/conferences, family/parent conferences/workshops, single adult "get togethers" and study groups are just a few openings for these needs of information, biblical assessment and feedback.

There are many well-informed, trained pastoral counselors, pastors, church staff personnel, seminary teachers, teachers in our Baptist colleges, and chaplains who are able to lead in the enriching and growing in strength aspects of who we are. The pulpit is an apt place to proclaim good news for living through situational preaching. There is how we can be helped and guided and know theological underpinnings from the Word of God. "Whatever happens, conduct yourselves in a manner worthy of the gospel of Christ" (Phil. 1:27, NIV). "Submit to one another out of reverence for Christ" (Eph. 5:21, NIV). Therefore, "Be very careful, then, how you live—not as unwise but as wise . . ." (Eph. 5:15, NIV).

What Are My Closer Relationships Like? If Angela and Chris have a healthy sense of who they are, they will begin to create stabilizing and freeing personal relationships. Intimacy may include these elements: firm loyalty to the other, mutual support and availability, a shared view of the world, mutual self-disclosure, and shared, honest vulnerability. Intimacy does involve friendship. It is not being equated with sexual relationships here.

By this time, Angela and Chris have experienced: strangers—acquaintances—friendships—intimacies. At one end, they know strangers, persons who are really neither for or against them. They have many acquaintances that are known casually and informally. Sometimes these persons move into friendship. The intimate persons are the ones who know them deeply, perhaps even some of their inmost secrets. Not all of your relationships should have intimacy as its goal. Intimate relationships need preserving in order not to be like an open-ended book to be read by just anyone.

Loneliness is the other side of friendship and intimacy. It is a very common experience in our culture and even in the sometimes crowded church. James Lynch in his book *The Broken Heart: The Medical Consequences of Loneliness* insists that persons who live alone are more susceptible than others to the likelihood of serious illness.

Let's notice how complicated and enriching our relationships can be. "How much of my day is absorbed in relating to other persons?" "Do I have several friends, and what kinds of closeness do I have with other persons?" "Where do these relationships generate—church, work, and so on?" "Is my life too crowded with people?" "Are there too few people in my life?" "Do I plan to get together with others that matter to me, or do I leave this to 'bump in' chances?" "What do I like and enjoy in other persons?" "Do I tend to need my friends more than they express need of me?" "How do others know I care for them?" "Do I take persons for granted?" "Do I allow others to care for me?" "Do I respect other persons?" "Am I willing to talk about myself appropriately with persons who convey closeness to me?" "Am I an active listener and not just a hearer and repeater of words?" "What does being close to someone mean to me?" "How do you get in touch with them?" "Who am I particularly close to currently?" "Does closeness tend to arouse my anxiety and awkwardness?" "How do I encourage special persons to get closer to me?" "Do people see me as a distant, controlled person, or a balanced feeling person?" "Do they experience my anger or frustration more than my consideration and warmth?" "How do I handle my feelings when I'm with others?" "Especially, how do I respond when I perceive I'm being turned away?" "Have I ever been/felt rejected?" "Am I disappointed easily?" "Do I seem to want a fair amount of give-and-take in these relationships?" "For instance, what would I feel comfortable asking my friends?" "Am I a healthy compromiser, or an unbending controller?" "Do I expect to be treated as 'an equal,' and also to treat my friends 'as equals'?" "How do I get along generally in my school, work, church, family relationships?" "Do I permit others to be themselves?"[23]

If you will take a few moments, write out your own definition of *intimacy.* Jesus' intimacy and friendship with the Father becomes the foundation of our friendships and trustworthy intimacies as Christians. "I and the Father are one" ("together"; see John 1:14-16). This issue enables us to share the power and nature of blessing with others in freedom.

What Are My Deeper Interpersonal Commitments? Vocational choice and marital choice are indeed two of the most significant decisions of a lifetime. They become major determinants of your personality development and perhaps the style of life that you lead. Sometimes they are decided smoothly; other times with a good bit of flip-flopping. Yet they are complex matters. At this point, if you are married, these might be helpful inquiries. "What is our marriage like?" "What did I expect to be happening?" "What kind of relationship do I have to my parents now?" A triad of meaning enters the picture: love, marriage, family. When? The marriage ceremony gives permission to be responsibly adult. Marriage anxieties and adjustments need healing time. The church can be a suitable facilitator of enrichment, awakening hope, and constructive problem solving.

Some general reflection exercises on the nature and meaning of commitment would include: (1) "When I say that I am committed to another person, I mean. . . ." (2) Focus on a close, committed person to you and write down the qualities that accent its special meaning. (3) Pursue this. "What do you suppose happens for some relationships to take on commitment whereas others do not?"

Commitment is a pledge to do something, a binding to a course of action, and a meaning to stand alongside of and with the other (Rom. 12:1). Commitment is to give oneself in trust. It gives a special flavoring to life. The Christian meaning of love involves responsiveness and commitment. Marriage is a visible, public, special commitment to responsibility before the creative Lord who "ordains" it. A committed young adult whether in friendship or in marriage does not live life in a "yes-but" style. The noncommitted person relies on a method of evasion that says yes and no at the same time. The committed person lets the yes be yes and the no be no. Commitment is the antithesis of alienation.[24]

There are some snag points that hinder wholehearted commitment: (1) a pervasive low sense of personal worth, (2) detachment from people, and (3) disenchantment with special causes or centers of focus. Oates further suggests that persons find it very hard to commit that which they do not value. The church's ministry can illustrate and recall its great, long-standing heritage of care and the learned wisdom of its experience. We are made in the image of God. We are persons for whom Christ died. We belong to the Living Lord and to a community of faith who care. Hopefully out of this caring context will come a valuing of ourselves as we recognize we are valued by God. (See 2 Cor. 1:17 to 22.)

Do I Deserve Leisuretime? In a workaholic, success-performance—highly productive—hurried oriented world, we need to reclaim leisure as grounded in the doctrine of creation. The work-rest rhythm appears basically in the fact God himself labored six days and rested on the seventh (Gen. 2:1-3). At the heart of leisure is the issue of freedom. One's time can be used creatively or confusingly. The use of time is a factor in leisure also.

In a very fine book *When You Can't Find Time for Each Other,* Wayne Oates confronts the common assertion by couples, family members, and singles that you are unable to find time for yourselves and for each other. He surfaces some of those hidden obstacles that delay you from choosing to discover time.

Pastoral strategy within the church can assess where it is adding to the problem of overuse of time related to activities and not enough balance of being still, serendipitous, and life celebrators who enjoy. It may be that the church needs to help persons to know how they presume at times upon the grace and love of their marriages and families. Look for the thieves of your time! One of the major tasks of the church is to provide guidelines, methods, and means for the best use of free time by its members in terms of ministering to the whole person. Leisure is a gift from God for a purpose, whether to be used for vacations, sports, hobbies, or whatever. For the glory of God. Thus, these activities can become opportunities for deeper commitment to Christ and involvement in serving Him.

Is My World Big Enough? Explain what comes to mind when you hear the term *citizen.* "What are the social organizations and institutions that you feel will have a necessary or important influence on you and/or your marriage/family in the years to come?" "Is there personal investment in the larger community beyond friends, work, marriage or family?" "Is it high, medium, low?" "Do I have genuine community, civic, political interests?" "Am I a *detractor,* impeding the group's goals/ work, a *mere member,* with nominal or little attention to what's going on, an *observer,* a *participant, contributor,* or *leader?*"[25]

One response is a selective inattention or naiveté—"Everything will be just fine"—and another is cynicism—"Everything is really corrupt or hopeless, so why bother." Young adults particular face the sandtrap of this "either—or."

The Lord expects us to be effective, faithful Christians who know how to be effective citizens with our eyes open, to live up to his calling in terms of responsible citizenship (see Romans 12:21 to 13:1; 14:17-19; Matt. 22:21).

Additional Principles of Pastoral Care

Laurence Peter's prescription for humor therapy seems to offer some ready-made proverbs for ministering in a quickly manageable way:

1.   Follow your doctor's advise.
2.   Acquire positive expectations of health.
3.   Laugh it up.[26]

Therefore, a paraphrase might read: "Follow the minister's advice; acquire positive expectations of spiritual well-being; and *enjoy.*" If only life happened in that gliding manner and we had that kind of proverbial influence over people! The metaphor from the poster I saw once might be a better starting place. "Walking isn't a lost art—one must, by some means, get to the garage." There is no "one way" to care for young adults. They may be single, married, or formerly married. However, we will try walking, getting to the garage, and other means to try to get in touch with them.

Learning the Laughter of Faith. Since so much voicing in our world dwells on the critical, the fearful, the sad, and the distorted, learning how to enhance and to harness our God-given creative powers to joy in life is an important task. Jonathan Swift's earlier summary for health care, "The best doctors in the world are Dr. Diet, Dr. Quiet, and Dr. Merryman," seems appropriate. Humor as a "first cousin" correlate to the meaning of joy is part of our reserve to handle our faith.

Albert Schweitzer once wrote that "each patient carries his own doctor inside him." Let's take some of that self-defeating energy and turn it to health. Laughter as a kind of "spiritual doctor" inside you brings about beneficial physiological results as well as spiritual energy to relieve stress, alleviate pain, and wipe out anger (compare, James 1:19-20; Eph. 4:20,26-32). Laughter exercises the lungs and stimulates the circulatory system. Norman Cousins in his bestselling *Anatomy of an Illness* called laughter "a form of internal jogging." It reduces muscle tension. Moreover, a sense or attitude of humor—not allowing things to get us down, the ability to see through our pretensions, the capacity to hope and to endure, and changing too high expectations—is related to a positive, enriching attitude and the will to live.

Indeed, a sense of humor enlarges our capacity to *relax* in order to renew strength and vision, to see the inconsistencies in our behavior, to resolve problems, to create our own mirth, to laugh at illness and crisis, and to communicate effectively. Peter's prescription for growing a sense of humor includes: (1) adopt an attitude of playfulness—it is OK to be silly at times, so give yourself healthy permission; (2) think funny; (3) laugh at yourself—not in derision, but in acceptance of the fact "I am unfinished. Here's a recent example"; and (4) take yourself "lightly."[27]

Unfortunately some have a view that religion and humor do not mix, because laughter is linked with "worldliness." But listen to Scripture: "The morning stars sang together, and all the sons of God shouted for joy" (Job 38:7). Spiritual life in Christ is an amazing, wondrous gift to be enjoyed. Perhaps George Buttrick with a wink in his eye is on track, "No somber God could ever have made a bullfrog or a giraffe."[28] I once had a student who responded to a discussion on the providential care of God by asking, "Does God ever smile for you—at you?"

The Gospel accounts of the birth of Jesus have joy (and rejoicing) as their common theme. Furthermore, "the Word became flesh and dwelt among us" (John 1:14) is the central affirmation of the New Testament. God has come close to us not as an enemy but as a Savior and friend (John 15:15). His message is redeeming, reconciling love. In a sense, we can laugh from relief. The laugh is one of amazement, delight, disbelief that he really does love us, and a faith that takes over with assurance. How else can we respond but to give back our shouts of joy and to "en-joy" his created things? Jesus said, prior to the Passion events, "Be of good cheer, I have overcome the world" (John 16:33).

Getting in Touch with Your Gift. Chris and Angela as persons—as young adults—are a kind of gift from God. Understanding their personhood as a gift is foundational to their Christian life. "How do they receive gifts?" "Are they thankful?" Life is not something that we create out of nothing. We really did not earn it. It is a gift through the processes and mystery of life given to our parents. Thurl Ravenscroft, the long-time voice character of Tony the Tiger on the Kellogg's ad for the Frosted Flakes cereal came one time to the college campus where I was chaplain. He was sharing the fact that he had major surgery that brought unexpected news many years ago. As he lay in his hospital bed wondering what was coming on next, he realized anew that his life was really a gift from God. He explored the options available in receiving a gift, such as: apathy, acting as if God wasn't involved in life; cynicism, a symbolic snubbing of God for the problems of suffering in the world; self-madeness, not feeling responsible to or needing anyone else; or finally thanksgiving, recognizing and claiming the gift. The proper response to a gift is indeed "thanks." There has never been anybody before us or anybody who will come after us who is exactly like us. My life as a gift? In Christ, life and life anew is an unexpressible gift, given by grace, not earned (Eph. 2:7-10).

The self-made concept, which the Pharisees of Jesus' day seemed to embody, is one that says, "You owe me! And what can you do for me? It is not, 'What can I give you?' But I have arrived!" Someone has suggested that the self-made person is one that really does not know how to say thanks or at least functions out of an inability to say it to those who have supported, taught, prayed for, befriended, guided, and stood by them.

Learning to reinforce our ability to say thanks to God for our lives is part of the teaching care of the young adult. I have learned that a thankful person is a hopeful person. Thankful persons tend to "esteem" their worth as children of God. Young adult, take hold of your gift with "thanks—living."

Developmental Layer	Pastoral Strategy/Program	Implementation Desired
"Leaving Home" 18-22	1. Educational/career/ vocational guidance and information, clarification /reorganizing values/ priority levels via questionnaires/ conferences	1. Well-fitting career decisions
		2. Claiming one's gift of life
	2. Personal growth and enrichment, building workshops-"taking hold of your gift" theme	3. Effective/informed social interacter/ responder-consumer
		4. Healthy homelife
		5. Worthy single
	3. Interpersonal- communication skills- groups	6. Crisis/problem solver
		7. Balanced and diverse stress management
	4. Homemaking-parenting workshops	8. Learning to delay gratification rather than demanding instant gratification
	5. Living by oneself-creative singles workshops	
	6. Time management/using gifts in ministry	9. Prayer/meditative life-style
	7. Stress without distress	10. Learning to say thanks (Col. 3:15-16)
	8. Life situation Bible study	
	9. Preparation/readiness for marriage/conferences	

Developmental Layer	Pastoral Strategy/Program	Implementation Desired
"Becoming Adult" 23-28	1. Neo-married/marriage retreats/groups	1. Effective growing marriages
(Some overlap of prior layer)	2. Parenting-child's esteem conferences	2. Occupational satisfaction
	3. Owning/Buying a home	3. Healthy, consistent parenting
	4. Living as a single/ formerly married conferences	4. Informed citizen
	5. Creative problem solving communication	5. Well-being in homelife
	6. Volunteer dynamics and leadership roles and "causes"	6. Confidence in where one is as single
		7. Enhancing problem solving abilities
	7. Coping with stress	8. Personal growth in handling transitional stress
"Catch 30"	1. Owning what is important/clarifying values/expectations	1. Examining/owning one's commitments/ "importances"
(The gap between leaving home and here begins to shape out)	2. Marriage Counseling/ enrichment groups- communication assessment workshops	2. Faithful personal relationships
	3. Parent-child concerns	3. Sense of achievement/ competence in one's work
	4. Consumer interests/ financial planning	4. Growth beneficial to parent-child interactions
	5. Crises groups-grief, formerly married, etc.	5. Responsible consumer behavior
	6. Problem solving negotiations	6. Appropriate problem solving/conflict negotiation
	7. Stress management	7. Personal growth in coping with life's changes

Notes

1. William J. Bouwma, *Adulthood,* ed. Erik Erikson (New York: W. W. Norton and Co., 1978), p. 85.

2. Theodore Lidz, *The Person* (New York: Basic Books, Inc., 1968), p. 362.

3. Ibid.

4. Virginia Satir, *Peoplemaking* (Palo Alto: Science and Behavior Books, Inc., 1972), p. 3.

5. Ibid., pp. 1-19.

6. Gerard Egan and Michael A. Cowan, *Moving into Adulthood* (Monterey, Calif.: Brooks/Cole Publishing Co., 1980).

7. Daniel J. Levinson, *The Seasons of a Man's Life* (New York: Alfred A. Knopf, Inc., 1978), p. 73.

8. Lucien E. Coleman, Jr., *Understanding Today's Adults* (Nashville: Convention Press, 1982), p. 91.

9. Egan and Cowan, pp. 11-17.

10. Levinson, pp. 90-111.

11. Egan and Cowan, p. 21.

12. Ronald W. Ramsay and Rene Noorbergen, *Living with Loss* (New York: William Morrow and Co., Inc., 1981), pp. 66-75.

13. Wayne Oates, *Your Particular Grief* (Philadelphia: The Westminster Press, 1981), p. 103.

14. Egan and Cowan, pp. 27-29.

15. Ibid., p. 32. See also Gerard Egan, *Exercises in Healing Skills.*

16. Vivian Rogers McCoy, Colleen Ryan, and James W. Lichtenberg, *The Adult Life Cycle: Training Manual and Reader,* (Lawrence: The University of Kansas, 1978), p. 229. See Appendix I for an adaptation of these tasks, programs outcomes sought to pastoral strategy.

17. These themes are derived from Egan and Cowan and will be used throughout to blend with pastoral care approaches.

18. Egan and Cowan, pp. 51ff.

19. Ibid., pp. 82-119.

20. Paul Pruyser, *The Minister as Diagnostician* (Philadelphia: The Westminster Press, 1976), pp. 62-67.

21. Egan and Cowan, pp. 236-53.

22. Ibid., pp. 154-74.

23. Ibid., pp. 185-212.

24. Wayne Oates, *The Psychology of Religion* (Waco: Word Books, Publishers, 1973), pp. 222-225.

25. Egan and Cowan, p. 259.

26. Lawrence J. Peter, *The Laughter Prescription* (New York: Ballantine Books, 1982), p. 11.

27. Ibid., p. 193.

28. George Buttrick, *Sermons Preached in a University Church* (New York: Abingdon Press, 1959), p. 52.

Additional Bibliography

Bagby, Daniel G. *Before You Marry.* Nashville: Convention Press, 1983.

Barnette, Henlee. *Has God Called You?* Nashville: Broadman Press, 1969.

Bruehl, Richard. "The Process of Leaving Home in a Case of Family Pastoral Counseling." *The Journal of Pastoral Care.* Vol. 25, No. 4 (Dec., 1971).

Clinebell, Howard J. *Growth Counseling for Marriage Enrichment: Pre-Marriage and the Early Years.* Philadelphia: Fortress Press, 1975.

Erikson, Erik (ed.). *Adulthood.* New York: W. W. Norton and Co., 1978.

Fowler, Jim and Sam Keen. *Life Maps: Conversations on the Journey of Faith.* Waco: Word Books, Publishers, 1980.

Hovde, Howard. *The Neo-Married.* Valley Forge: The Judson Press, 1968.

Lawson, Linda (comp.). *Working With Single Adults in Sunday School.* Nashville: Convention Press, 1978.

Lester, Andrew D. *Coping With Your Anger: A Christian Guide.* Philadelphia: The Westminster Press, 1983.

Mace, David and Vera. *How to Have a Happy Marriage.* Nashville: Abingdon, 1977.

Oates, Wayne. *Christ and Selfhood.* New York: Association Press, 1961.

—————. *When You Can't Find Time for Each Other.* St. Meinrad, Ind.: Abbey Press, 1982.

Pinson, William M., Jr. *The Biblical View of the Family.* Nashville: Convention Press, 1981.

Sheehy, Gail. *Passages: Predictable Crises of Adult Life.* New York: E. P. Dutton and Co., Inc., 1976.

Swindoll, Charles R. *Three Steps Forward Two Steps Back.* Nashville: Thomas Nelson Publishers, 1980.

Tubesing, Donald A. *Kicking Your Stress Habits.* Duluth, Minnesota: Whole Person Associates, Inc., 1981.

5
The Middle Years: On the Go!
George H. Gaston, III

The intriguing drama of life moves into the middle stages of adult-hood somewhere between the ages of 35 and 40. Individuals who arrive at this plateau of existence embark upon life's potentially longest and perhaps most difficult phase. Those persons who live to encounter the challenges of the senior adulthood will spend approximately 20 to 25 years in these mid-ranges of life. The numerous battles which must be encountered can best be described as painful opportunities calling for determination and persevering hope.

The middle adult years are not a time for settling down. Those theorists who seek to paint the canvas of mid-life as a season simply for enjoying the fruits of one's labor miss the dynamism of this time. Even those middle-age warriors who have an abundance of life's comforts and securities are faced with the internal dilemmas which life invariably thrusts upon its participants. The middle adult years truly are years "on the go." In preparation for the latter phases of human existence, the person must work through the developmental concerns of being in the middle.

Individuals do not arrive at this new occasion for maturing as empty vessels or blank tablets. They are the products of over thirty-five years of living. Whatever they have gained from their family experience, culture, education, friendships, crises, vocation, and religion will influence their capacity for traveling through the middle years. Some will approach this time as crippled soldiers, ill-equipped for the difficulties to be faced. Lacking in a strong sense of personal strength, they will stumble and fall over the threats to their finitude. On the other hand, those who have been immersed in relationships of love and appropriate security will respond with a spirit of faith and hope, even though at times they will stumble. This reality, coupled with the uniqueness of

each person, dictates that every individual will approach quite differently the middle of life.

Much has been published on the whole of life's journey and the early
and late phases of our humanity, but little has been dedicated to the
crisis of the in-between. Groundbreaking works such as Daniel J. Levinson's *The Seasons of a Man's Life* and the popular *Passages: Predictable
Crises of Adult Life* by Gail Sheehy have helped us to gain a foothold on
this large slice of life.[1]

Those of us who minister to human need through the church should
look carefully into such research for clues and directional signals on
caring for the mid-life person. The gap which exists in the church's
understanding of and ministry to the mid-life person is obvious. We are
perplexed by the traumas which come in the lives of median adults but
have not much in the way of innovative and helpful ministry for these
persons. We focus our energy on the young who are preparing for life
and sometimes forget that life is a continual process of preparation.
Hopefully, this chapter will add to the much-needed discussion on
ministry to these needy pilgrims as we explore what it means to be an
adult in mid-life.

Developmental Theorists

Scholars who have analyzed the mid-life experience have labeled the
growth tasks of this time-frame in a variety of ways. Consistently, however, the issue which is presented as the key growth challenge of
mid-life resembles the biblical call to faith. Their writings do not always
discuss the person of God or the ways of the gospel, but they have seen
in persons an unavoidable questing in the mid-time of life for the
meaning of life and ways to make life a richer experience.

L. J. Sherrill

Lewis Joseph Sherrill wrote an intriguing little volume entitled *The
Struggle of the Soul*. This man of faith described a scheme of life which
involved five major phases: childhood, adolescence, young adulthood,
middle adulthood, and the senior adult experience. Sherrill's book was
a keystone in the process of teaching many young seminary students the
developmental nature of life. The book challenged them to trace the
life of faith from childhood to old age.

Sherrill explored five struggles which coincided with the stages of life: becoming an individual, being weaned away from parents, finding one's basic identifications in life, achieving a mature view of life and the universe, and developing a simplified view of life so that the soul may proceed on to its chosen destiny. The description of a mid-life struggle, achieving a mature view of life and the universe, was set forth in terms of mankind's need to find meaning in life and live for the lasting values. Achieving such a view of life and universe was analyzed by Sherrill in terms of developing a philosophy of life that helps the person to discover the essence of all life. He wrote:

> In this matter of a philosophy of life it is quite possible that we are dealing with an activity of the mind which is exactly as instinctual as growth itself. For the making of a philosophy of life is the self striving to relate, not to parts, but to the whole. It is striving to relate, not now merely to persons, or things, or to society and the flux of human events, or the world of adult life; but rather to the totality of all that has been, or is now, or ever shall be.[2]

Sherrill was correct in noting that not all persons develop a philosophy of life that is clearly pointed in the direction of self-giving. Even so, the struggle to understand the nature and purpose of life takes place in adults during mid-life. Hopefully, they come to see the truly important things that help life open up into the fullness which existence holds for all who will obediently trust and journey onward in flexibility, integrity, and relationship.

Daniel J. Levinson

Daniel J. Levinson projected a theory of adult development for males that is based in a psychological perspective. In *The Seasons of a Man's Life,* Levinson identifies the developmental task of mid-life transition as questioning life's structure. For some, the transition is quite severe, causing the development of what Levinson labels a mid-life crisis. As a man moves through his transition (or crisis), he must come to terms with the values and processes of his life. In the final analysis of things, the person must alter either his value system, the approach to his work, the structure and approach to his family life, or all of these. In effect, a man moving through mid-life is rebuilding his life. He asks himself such questions as the following: "What have I done with my life? What do I really give to and receive from my spouse, children, work, friends, community, and self? What is it I truly want from myself and others?"[3]

Like Sherrill, Levinson seems to postulate that the mid-life transition struggle is based in the mere fact of chronological aging. As persons become older, they automatically move through the inevitable transitions of existence. Levinson is similar to Sherrill in his articulation of the developmental struggle at mid-life in terms of meaning and approach to life. Both theorists have stated that man is a creature who comes at the mid-point to ask questions about the purpose of existence. Once this struggle has begun to be resolved, the person can go on to live out the fullness of the middle years and beyond.

Gail Sheehy

Akin to Levinson's work is that of Gail Sheehy, *Passages: Predictable Crises of Adult Life.* Based in part upon the work of Levinson, Sheehy identified the middle-age development issue as being that of growing simultaneously on three basic adult frontiers: work, relationships to significant others, and the relationship to oneself. Her thesis emphasized the importance of persons groping toward authenticity. She declared:

> It is for each of us to find a course that is valid by our own reckoning. And for each of us there is the opportunity to emerge reborn, authentically unique, with an enlarged capacity to love ourselves and embrace others.[4]

Sheehy sees the middle thirties as being the literal mid-point of life, a time, "if we let ourselves," to have a "full-out authenticity crisis."[5]

The work which Sheehy has done fits nicely beside that of both Sherrill and Levinson. She, too, understands persons to be dealing with the meaning of all things, attempting to find a mature, acceptable approach to living as an adult. The mid-life individual begins to have a changing sense of time, a growing desire truly to be alive, a reappraisal of self and others, and a reframing of life's priorities.

Erik Erikson

One of the most significant theorists for an understanding of mid-life is Erik Erikson. Erikson's eight stage psychosocial framework on the development of man is renown. He focused the median adult development crisis around two polarities: generativity and stagnation or self-absorption. The middle-age person seeks to develop a sense of generativity without giving over to the debilatating process of stagnation and self-absorption. For Erikson, this issue is ethical in nature. He suggested that the matter is not so much an item related to chronological development as it is related to the ethical virtue of care. As an individual arrives at a point in life when he has established relationships, children, vocation, and values, he must then decide if he is to care for that which he has generated. *Generativity,* a word coined by Erikson, means to care about and for the future by investing something of yourself in nurturing those persons, causes, and values which will go on after you and will aid in some small way to make the planet earth a better place for the offspring of the human family. Fundamentally, generativity has to do with establishing and growing the next generation of humanity.

Erikson emphasized the necessity of getting under the load of life. The middle-age adult who refuses this challenge is the person who slips into the stagnation of self-absorption. The truth is, each mid-lifer is caught somewhere between generativity and stagnation. Some arenas of life will be filled with generativity, others will know the pain of stagnant waters. The consistent challenge is to move toward generativity.

The Mid-Life Issue: A Summary

The issue confronting the person in mid-life is that of deciding to live the life of faith. In particular, the struggle is one of determining who one is, what one needs to be doing in life, and where one wants to plant his life. It is a concern which is brought on by the passing of years and the arrival of the person at a responsible level of being. Somewhere in the thirties and forties, when a person has put down some roots, tasted a measure of achievement, and begun to realize the unreachable parts of life, the mid-life struggle unfolds in earnest. The person begins to move toward a mature philosophy of life.

Theologically speaking, all of this is born of the Holy Spirit. It is He who meets us all along the road of life and calls us onward to the next plateau of being. God is at work in the median adult, asking for an evaluation of one's priorities and life goals. No matter that a person does not acknowledge His presence. The calling to faith and life is from Beyond. The temptation to stagnate and become self-absorbed dates back to the Garden of Eden and mankind's fall. Those who will hear

His voice and move forward to live with authenticity, generativity, and responsibility will discover the full reward of life's deepest joy.

As one who is called to minister to middle-age sojourners, you must be alert to the overarching developmental concern at midpoint in life. Learn to see the afternoon people as those who are going through something of an identity crisis. View them as philosophers who are asking questions which go to the core of life. Your temptation will be to miss the big issue through being snared in the webb of smaller issues which compose the day-to-day existence of the median. You will want to equip yourself as the kind of helper who knows how to guide them through the unavoidable maze of struggles which they confront on their way to a mature philosophy of life.

Temptations to Stagnation: Issues Along the Way

What are the life issues which confront median adults and tempt them toward stagnation? What causes them to begin questioning life and evaluating the way they have lived life? Now that the big picture has been sketched, attention will be given to the particular matters which give rise to the philosophical dilemma of the middle-adult experience. An understanding of these consistent hurdles which loom in the middle of the race is essential. They are the concrete opportunities by which the median individual will either develop generativity or stagnation.

Bodily Processes

At some point in a person's late twenties, the body ceases to wax and starts to wane. Time takes its toll on the magnificent human body. That which once seemed indestructible, now at mid-life begins to show signs of obvious change and unavoidable decline. As a result, persons begin to develop a subtle sensitivity and lack of confidence in the ability of their bodies to perform in ways previously assumed possible. Wrinkling, sagging skin; graying, receding hair; cracking, stiff joints; drooping, growing hips and stomachs; and weakening, flabby muscles all begin to pump fear into the heart of an adult. They are some of the first signs of life's changing realities.

The fact that man is viewed biblically as a unified being (not to be divided into unrelated parts such as body, mind, and soul) helps us understand the reason bodily changes are often traumatic to the individual. The body is an expression, in part, of who a person is. Identity is bound up in physical appearance. Hence, when the body begins to move toward an obvious pattern of aging, the person begins to face the finitude of humanity. Such awareness can be most threatening. Increased efforts to keep the body young are often employed. Many persons cope with bodily changes through jesting. A recent cartoon quipped: "As I approach middle-age, I'm developing a bad problem, my shirts and I taper in different directions." Bob Hope is attributed with having defined middle-age as that time of life "when your age starts to show around your middle."[6] How good it is to laugh about ourselves! Nonetheless, even the jokes we tell speak of our aging anxiety. Laughter eases some of the tension.

In America, the process of aging is complicated by living in a culture which deifies physical beauty and derides the aged. Oriental cultures are known for their reverential treatment of the mature. Such is not the case in Western society. The American advertising industry flaunts the qualities of youth and promotes products which will slow the bodily aging process. Athletes and beauty queens seem to be the folk heroes of our day. Serious questions about self-worth are continually raised by many median adults who are unable to convince their bodies not to show age. Is it any wonder that mid-life persons often try to find renewal for their lives through becoming workaholics or venturing into a sea of irresponsible living searching for affirmation? Has the church added to this problem by elevating the virtues of strength, beauty, and youth over those of maturity, experience, and wisdom?

Goals of Life

A second matter which mid-life adults must encounter is an emotional tussle over reaching the goals of life which one has established. Establishing goals for living seems to be a natural phenomenon among persons. Not all of our goals are established in openness or formulated with intentionality. Even so, in some way all persons will formulate the images and dreams of successful life which will guide the direction and intensity of their living. Goals might be traced to a person's childhood. Parents may subtly give to their children the visions for life which they were unable to accomplish. For instance, the nebulous goal of being wealthy often stems from a family that struggles through many rough years "trying to make ends meet." Many of the objectives which adolescents and young adults set for themselves are rooted in these vague desires of childhood.

Not all of life's visions are traceable to fuzzy beginnings. Persons are constantly working with the crises of development, making decisions about who they are becoming, and setting goals for where they are going in life. Life priorities also stem from one's religious encounters, educational processes, and the awareness of needs which are present in society.

What does all of this have to do with mid-life? By the time a person reaches the middle, many of life's pursuits have been accomplished; many will never be attained. Both realities can prove to be perplexing. A thirty-six-year-old dentist brags and laments: "I've already accomplished everything I set out to do. Where do I go from here?" A forty-year-old mother of four children begins to understand that her offspring aren't going to become the "successful" persons she had dreamed them to be, and she senses herself to be a failure. Medians who decide to change careers, go back to school, or move to another place often do so in an effort to relieve the internal tensions which come with the struggle over life's goals.

The middle-adult experience is a time for feeling the pangs of failure and guilt over life goals. Likewise, it is an occasion for feeling lost at the top with no further mountains to be climbed. Hopefully, this season of existence can be one of the most creative times of life. As one faces and accepts the limitations of life, going through the process described by Sheehy as the "de-illusionment of our dreams," one is able to set goals which are more realistic.[7] The successful feelings which attend the accomplishment of sought-after dreams should be the fuel that sets persons on their way toward different and new horizons. Many who grow stagnant in the middle of life do so for lack of a guide who points the way beyond guilt, frustration, and realized success. Surely the church and her ministers of concern will want to serve as agents who equip and guide persons on their way to the City of Abraham's faith.

Letting Go of Responsibilities

Another threatening development for the middle-age individual who has enjoyed taking hold of life's handles and making the process work is the ascent of humanity's next generation. Not long after a person begins to feel comfortable with power, there comes the realization that others are standing nearby asking for the privilege of sharing the power. If the median adult will look carefully, he can see himself in the eyes of the young ones who have arrived on the scene. Such awareness can be quite disconcerting. It reminds the mid-lifer that he is aging. "Where has the time gone?" Only "yesterday" the one in the middle was making the right moves to take hold of the power. And now, someone younger wants the median adult to release and share a portion of the power.

An inevitable struggle is set in motion when a person's perceived power base is threatened. Human beings don't give up their territory with ease. Created to have dominion and to subdue the earth, we doggedly stake out our areas of responsibility. The powerful deception of our sinful nature causes us to desire ownership and ultimate control. We lose sight of the God-given reality that life is to be lived as stewards (overseers) of the process and not despots. Life, however, has a way of reminding us of our stewardship. Mid-life persons quite often find it difficult to bless the sharing of power.

Pastors will sense this real battle in the lives of their parishioners as they take note of the marked increase in median adult apathy and withdrawal. Their countenance often cries out, "What's the use!" Consistently, the struggle can be seen in the way medians begin to compete for their role of leadership in the church. Anger will be on the increase with some. They may determine to "hold onto things the way they've 'always' been." Change becomes increasingly difficult. Mid-life people at times tend to dig a frontline trench and hold off the onslaught of the aggressor. Unless this mentality is addressed in the church, adults will slip deeply into the reality of stagnation and self-absorption. They must be helped in the task of joining hands with the wide generations of life. They stand in the middle of life, and in such a position are an indispensable link between the generations of mankind.

Changing Relationship Structures

By the time a person reaches the middle experience of life, a webb of relationships has been established. These are vitally important contacts of existence. In these communal entities of meaning, individuals are nurtured into life. Some of their relationships stretch back to the cradle. Others are recent additions to the person's support structure. As the person has dared to interact with these sojourners, identity and life's purpose have come into focus. The stability of these relationships is crucial for the person's well-being and sense of hope for life. Because this is true, one of the most trying parts of mid-life is found in the multiple changes which happen in the support structure of every median adult. Some mid-life theorists believe the most difficult part of living through the middle is found in the instability of relationships. Every relationship which has helped to form the person will be tested, altered, or permanently lost during the years of middle adulthood.

1. *Aging Parents.*—One of the changing relationships which is most demanding on the middle-age adult is the one many of them share with their aging parents. Parents who have lived to be senior adults present their mid-life children with increased life support needs. Not only must mid-life persons care for their own immediate families, but they must begin now to have an expanded role of care and attention for the parents who nurtured them into life. The extent of the care which is necessary varies. Monetary provisions, shared dwellings, daily visits, occasional contacts, and ongoing advocacy on their behalf are a few examples of the ways an individual might invest time in the care of aging parents.

For many persons in mid-life, the care of parents is a labor of love. Some are quite resistant to this need, however. Life for them has become complicated and they are too tired to provide the necessary nurture. Instead, they pull away from their parents. Those who are willing to take up the work of aiding an aging loved one must pay a significant price. The emotional strain which such care potentially adds to the mid-lifer and his family is not imaginary. The task of moving a senior adult into a mid-life household can be complicated, especially if adolescent family members are involved.

Throughout the process of caring for parents a temptation toward stagnation can be taking place within the mid-life adult. The investment of care in this new, and perhaps unexpected, responsibility may force the mid-lifer to sense a hopeless feeling of "I'll never get out from under this responsibility." If the person is still maneuvering for success and recognition, the addition of more family will be weighty.

2. *Adolescence.*—Another relationship which begins to change in the middle years is with children who grow through adolescence and leave home. The problems related to this issue are legion. Adolescents are persons with whom it is always challenging to live. The dynamic

changes through which they move are difficult to catalogue. These youthful years are a time for identity searching and questing for a direction in life. Interestingly enough, the developmental issue of adolescence is a reasonable facsimile of the issue which the mid-life individual is working to resolve. The crises through which the adolescent moves often aggravate the searching process of the mid-life parents with whom they are living. Parents may become resentful of their risky, questing teenager. The youthful strength and general attitude of challenging authority may prove to be a frustrating burden for parents who are experiencing their own transition of meaning.

In time, the teenager will move away from home and a totally new struggle will begin for the parent. As much discomfort as the adolescent development may cause, most often it is not to be compared with the shock of the "empty nest." Teenagers may leave home under the best of circumstances, or the worst. Parents will either be thrilled or dejected over the manner in which the child leaves and the style of life which their offspring chooses to adopt. Whatever their feelings, always there is the unavoidable process of reordering life without the adolescent. Even though an empty nest signals increased freedom for the median adult, with each departing young one there is the growing awareness of silence and emptiness. One "empty nest median" described the leaving of the last "chick" as an event which turned their home into "an empty cavern."

After years of nurturing children toward the goal of self-discipline and independence, parents must come to the awareness that, for better or worse, their task has been completed. They now move into a new time and relationship with their children. Hopefully, the time will come when they will stand side by side with their children as friendly equals in the world of responsible adulthood. For some parents, the joy of seeing their children arrive at such a state of full responsibility will be postponed. Their children will live out a prolonged adolescence, and, as parents, they must go through the torture of aiding them in the seemingly endless process of clearing one crisis after another. Their empty nest pain is frustrated by the guilt of feeling "we are failures." Failure to come to terms with this changing relationship with one's children can cause a depleted spirit.

3. *Marital Adjustments.*—One of the jolting realities often faced in mid-life is the awareness that the marital relationship around which

one's family has been built is now in disarray. The stress of making a living, coping with parents and children, and working through one's own emotional transitions can bring damage into the fiber of a marriage. Hence, another changing relationship of mid-life is found in one's marriage. Not every mid-life marriage will experience a severe decline in relational effectiveness. Many maturing marriages are sturdy. Statistical data gathered from studies of marriages in the middle years, however, indicate the decay which can consume unattended relationships. Howard Clinebell wrote concerning the problems facing mid-years couples:

> The "living happily ever after" myth is revealed as a patent fallacy in many mid-year marriages. Approximately one-fourth of the over one million couples who divorce each year in the United States have been married fifteen years or more. In the last five years, divorce among couples married twenty years or more has increased fifty percent. Most studies of marriages show a gradual disenchantment and a declining degree of marital satisfactions, especially for women, through the child-rearing years. The emotional distancing which occurs during these years often becomes permanent unless outside help is sought.[8]

Marriages cannot survive apart from the healthy environment which is created by the miracle of dialogue, flexibility, commitment, and the investment of time. Many mid-lifers suddenly awaken as marital strangers. Such is one of the frightening realities of growing into the median ranges of life. The sage advice of an elderly Baptist layman seems appropriate for every marriage: "Don't forget to make a life while you are making a living." And yet, so many do forget!

Coping with the changes which come and the inevitable stresses in marriage is a primary task of mid-life. Inability to do so will thrust the median into a posture of stagnation and inwardness. Not uncommon in the mid-years are stories of extramarital affairs, over-involvement in a social life, the beginnings of alcohol or drug dependency, and workaholism. All of these may be indicators of the stagnation which has infected mid-life individuals and their marriage.

Of course, not every middle-age person is married. Some have chosen singleness as a way of life. Others are single as a result of circumstances thrust upon them by life. The fact of their singleness does not relieve them of the need for intimate, supportive relationships of life. Just as the married median must invest considerable energy in making marriage a relationship of productivity, the single adult must also nurture healthy relationships. What a tragedy to arrive at the middle of life as a loner! The stagnant single adult in mid-life will need to move toward developing friendships. They, too, will face the battle of losing relationships of intimacy.

4. *Vocational Alterations.*—The relationship which one has to a vocation is also in transition during the mid-life growth period. Like the other crises which have entered the individual's experience, this changing relationship brings on anxiety. Few individuals move through mid-life without fantasizing, planning, trying, or actualizing a change in life's work. Tired of the same routine, many persons determine at the middle of life to try a different approach to work which will afford them a sense of freshness and challenge. The dream which was subdued years ago now may find a way to become reality. Some of this is brought on by the pressures of one's current work. Confusion in other areas of life also can feed the desire to make changes in vocational expression. Unable to breed a vital spirit into family, friendships, or one's personal life, work may be altered as a way of discovering exhilarating life.

Mid-life persons often make radical changes in profession and vocation. Bureaucracy and schedules may give way to cows, dirt, and open spaces. The risk of "going it alone" seems worth it for those who are tired of being responsible to someone else. The reevaluation of one's gifts and abilities at mid-life may send some back to school to prepare belatedly for the task they "should have been doing all along." Gale Sheehy calls those who move out on new vocational ventures at mid-life "pathfinders."[9] There is something intriguing about those who make a successful transition. However, not all mid-life work transitions are pleasant.

Some alterations in vocation are made out of force and not choice. Divorce and the death of a spouse can cause a shift in one's work. Employers who find certain mid-life personnel to be expendable may replace them with a younger, more aggressive individual. The rise and fall of local and national economies can force vocational transitions. Individual health and financial problems also spawn work changes. Circumstances such as these may prove to be a debilitating discouragement. Even pathfinders find their faces dirtied from the many falls which they take upon an uneven pathway. It is not easy to change one's work, voluntarily or otherwise. Grief and anxiety may be prominent emotions for those who go through the changing relationship of work. Depression may become an accepted daily countenance. Hopefully, the joy of renewal in life's calling becomes a reality.

5. *Changing Friendships.*—One final relationship change needs to be noted. In the mid-years, the changing of one's intimate friendship structure is inevitable. Friends that have walked through the celebrations and valleys with the mid-lifer begin to change. Trusted support persons move; others divorce; still others radically alter their life philosophy and drift away idealogically. Death begins to claim some. Loneliness and distance can mark the lives of many middle-age adults.

Who needs friends anyway? The answer, of course, is all of us. They are a vital part of the human support and growth system. Mid-lifers must be in a consistent state of developing friendships, both new and old. We need the nurture which comes in having those outside the family who accept us as we are and encourage us in the business of becoming all we can be. The risk of moving close to others must become a learned process for the median adult. Even if they have lived fairly secluded lives up until this point in their existence, they need the security of other comrades in the shifting sand of their current transition.

This is not an easy task to perform, especially if one is married. The situation is made even more difficult if children are still in the homes of median adults. Friendships are nurtured in the soil of common interests, similarity in life-styles, and the investment of time. The caring pastor and congregation will seek to be a friend. Also, they will help the community of faith to fulfill one of its most important functions, that of building relationships within the family of God. "Two are better than one, because they have a good reward for their toil. For if they fall, one will lift up his fellow; but woe to him who is alone when he falls and has not another to lift him up" (Eccl. 4:9-10, RSV).

A Summation: Tempted and Tried

Changes, changes, changes! That is, in part, what mid-life is all about. On every hand, the middle-age adult is confronted with the reality of change. Each change is a temptation to stumble into a state of ungenerative living. Physical changes, changes in the goals and objectives of one's life, alterations in relationships, and a restructuring of life's power system all are threats to generativity and faith. Living by faith will not come easy for the one who dares to be authentic and generate life's important values to the following generation. The grief, anger, depression, frustration, fear, and guilt which can mark the person who journeys through the struggle of developing and living out a mature philosophy of life must be dealt with appropriately. Hope, love, faith, health, self-discipline, flexibility, forgiveness, and enthusiasm must fill the heart of the middle-age person. Finding these treasures of grace is the key to turning the mid-point of life into some of life's most creative years. Pastoral care for the people who walk in this journey of becoming must focus on pointing the way to these indispensable keystones of life.

Ministering in the Middle

How then shall we care for these persons who are on the go throughout the afternoon of their pilgrimage? They are some of the most difficult people to reach with the message and ministry of the gospel. Those individuals and families who have already found great security in the church will tend to be most responsive to the input of the church and the pastor. Others will at times be suspect of caring initiative which invades their sometimes painful territory. The church and Christianity may be viewed as burdensome responsibilities which will place even greater demands on their time. The pastor could be perceived as a hovering parental/authority figure who only wants to limit their quest for happiness and fulfillment.

The distance which medians at times place between themselves and others can be an intimidating factor in initiating pastoral care. Folks in the middle can appear to be powerful, self-assured, angry, disinterested, busy, and withdrawn all in an effort to resist help. The bombardment of change which they are enduring may cause them to fear any further risk. The very thing which they need, a growing faith, may be the reality they most resist. The known quantity of their struggle may seem better than the unknown of the gospel.

As You Begin

Several theological issues concerning ministry to the middle-age person need to be faced while formulating an approach to caring for this age group. The caring/healing processes of life are not free to do their most powerful work if the theology which undergirds ministry is inaccurate. The following issues are pivotal for mid-life ministry.

1. *Life Is a Struggle.*—You can believe it. Life *is* a struggle. A preacher once summed up life as a process that gets better and better while it gets harder and harder. Those who would care for the median adults must absolve themselves of all notions that the life of faith will be one victorious experience after another. The temptations of Jesus (see Matt. 4:1-11) are illustrative of the journey called life. The tempter confronts us along the way with the misconception that life can be lived via the shortcut.

There is a struggle involved in being a median adult. Do not promise an easy way to the median. Each one will cope quite differently through the process of maturing. Your ministry cannot take on the guise of being a deliverer who can take the median out of the struggle. At best, you can help the mid-life person to make decisions to live by faith, point them in the direction of God, and encourage them when they stumble.

Pain and struggle must be viewed by the minister as opportunity for growth. Let the words of Paul guide you at this point: "We rejoice in our sufferings, knowing that suffering produces endurance, and endurance produces character, and character produces hope, and hope does not disappoint us, because God's love has been poured into our hearts through the Holy Spirit which has been given to us" (Rom. 5:3-5, RSV). Victory and joy are the by-products of faith. As one journeys toward the fulfillment of life, one finds that the fullness of heaven is at hand!

2. *Failure Isn't Always the Product of Error and Sin.*—How easy it is to label every failure as being rooted in some past sin or misguided action. No doubt, the medians with whom you work will feel a deep sense of past failures for their present dilemmas. Some of their struggles are directly rooted in poor management of life and bad decision making. We are the products of our past in so many ways. However, there is fallacy in assuming that all present struggle is the result of a miserable past. Job in the Old Testament is a good example of a man who reaped out of proportion to his sinful ways. His "ministers' " efforts to tie his current poor standings to the past were ill-advised.

Take care not to make this common assumption. The generativity necessary for productive living among medians will be found, in part, as you help them to understand that all of their problems cannot be traced to the past. Help your parishioners to accept and confess their real guilt, turning to live in true repentance. Then, guide them in seeing that some of their guilt is not appropriate and real.

3. *Sin Can Be Forgiven.*—Remember, regardless of how dark the night may become for those who are searching after generativity and mature faith, there is always grace and hope. The mess which we humans make of life seems to be most messy in mid-life. This is true, in part, because those in the middle have become involved in so much of life. They have accumulated relationships, power, and commitments. Their failures seem to affect and damage so many persons. As a result, the church often does not know how to respond. The pain involved in ministering to so much trauma can be intimidating and produce within us a resistance to minister. Perhaps we are afraid that their distress will contaminate us. In actuality, rather than being contaminated, we will discover that our efforts to reach the middle-age adult in their need will reap positive results.

Following a difficult extramarital sexual affair, a man in his forties considered the prospect of dropping away from church. Word about his involvement had spread through the community. People were shocked, hurt, and disappointed. He resigned from his positions in his church. A two-week separation occurred between the man and his spouse of nearly thirty years. Through determination, encouragement from friends, and counseling, they were able to reunite and go to work on rebuilding their lives. They began to come again to church. Before long, new rays of generativity began to blossom. After a long period of reentry to the family of faith, the man started to find ways of serving again in the church. In response to the question "How did you make it?" he replied, "God's grace and the church people just wouldn't leave me alone." Forgiveness is always a possibility! Sin can be forgiven—indeed, it has already been forgiven in the person of Jesus Christ! Can the church do any less? Mid-life ministry involves a theology of forgiveness. "Lord, how often must we forgive?" "Seven times seventy!" (see Matt. 18:21-22).

Such is not to say that we take lightly the process of sin. The God of life cannot abide the brokenness which destroys life. Pastors and churches will need to appropriately confront and challenge the confusion which threatens to mutilate the work of the Kingdom. Exerting pastoral initiative toward the ones who are guilty is never easy, but it must be accomplished. However, even in the midst of discipline the sounds of amazing grace should be heard.

4. *You Have a Ministry to Perform.*—How easy it is to lose sight of one's calling and authority with certain groups of folks and in some situations in life. Unsure of themselves, ministers may find themselves in retreat. One of the groups with which this happens most often is median adults. We are pushed away by their struggle. We begin to question our "right" to stand with them in their need. Nagging fears about our ability to deal with the enormous complexities of ministry may become full-blown panic in the presence of mid-life problems.

Coming to terms with one's calling and the source of one's personal power is a never-ending issue for ministry. Ministers must understand their own developmental struggles, stay in touch with a community of support which nurtures their sense of being, and live in the power of God's sustaining presence.[10] "God did not give us a spirit of timidity but a spirit of power and love and self-control" (2 Tim. 1:7, RSV). You have a right to express your ministry, you have been empowered for the ministry, and median adults need you.

Nurturing an Atmosphere of Hope

The beginning place for ministering to the needs of medians is through the development of an atmosphere of hope in your congregation. As a minister of the gospel, you operate against the backdrop of a local congregation. Most often, the people of mid-life who need your particular ministry are members of your congregation. One of the great strengths which you have to offer them (as well as those outside the congregation) is the support and environment of a covenant community. You minister as a representative of a local congregation.[11] In order for your work with medians to be as effective as possible, you must nurture your congregation into a community that radiates the spirit of hope. In that context, your personal ministry will be hope-filled.

How does a congregation communicate hope? It does so by living in a spirit of generativity. A generative church cares about what happens in the world and is looking for ways to carry on the good news of God's salvation. Congregations will radiate a positive spirit of hope as they generate the truth. Those bodies of believers that have lost a sense of mission will not have an atmosphere of hope and encouragement. Hence, they will probably not have a helpful ministry to median adults. Middle-age adults who are discouraged and stagnant will be encouraged to generate by being around others who are living with a spirit of generating hope.

The pastor plays a key role in the generation of hope in a church. You will want to lead your congregation to live out the truth in a risky fashion. Help them to understand the penetrating call of the gospel to go into the world with the love of Christ. Challenge them to invest in community missions which are needed. Lead them into mission causes which are far greater than your congregation, those that are worldwide in scope. To accomplish this style of churchmanship, congregations must begin to reevaluate styles of church life which seek to turn the church into a closed society. The church of Jesus Christ has always been most valuable when it lost itself in the world. Congregations wishing to be generative must ask themselves if they are serving only their kind of people, or if they are truly risking themselves with a whole world. The ever-present temptation in many congregations is to become self-serving rather than servants to a hungry, lonely world. We must remember the words of Christ, "Inasmuch as ye have done it unto one of the least of these my brethren, ye have done it unto me" (Matt. 25:46). The added benefit which comes in leading a congregation to be mission minded is the encouragement which such a posture of love builds up with median-age adults who experience the church's ministry through your pastoral work.

Teach a Christian Philosophy of Generativity

Another facet of ministry to middle-age persons is to be found in teaching them the truth about mid-life. Folks in the middle need some information about this time of life. They need to know how to navigate through these uncharted waters. By now, most Americans have come to know the term *mid-life crisis*, but few know the content of the idea. We have all heard the myths which grow out of our human adventures into the wilds of middle-life, but who can tell for sure what it is really like?

The pastor can help through his teaching ministry. He is not the only one who teaches in the congregation, but his central role as pastor-teacher puts him in a unique position to influence the entire teaching program of the church. For one thing, the pastor's sermons need to reflect sensitivity to middle-adult life. The realities of the median-adult experience should be addressed specfically through the sermonic format. The possibility of preaching a series on the life cycle holds great merit.[12] Also, the various teachings of most sermons could be applied specifically to the challenges of mid-life, as well as to the other phases of life.

In addition to sermons, the pastor can lead in developing church classes which identify the mid-life task and develop the life-skills needed for living as adults. No doubt, many pastors will lack the specific training and study in mid-life issues to teach with confidence such a course. Enlisting the teaching services of a gifted mid-life theorist might encourage the participation of your median adults. Potential topics for discussion with the adults would be: developing a philosophy for living as a mature adult; living with aging parents; growing with your teenager; when death comes at mid-life; making the most of your vocation; family life for middle-age adults; and the median adult in the church. An excellent book study for adults might be Reuel Howe's stimulating volume, *The Creative Years,* or William Hulme's *Mid-life Crisis.*[13]

Another teaching opportunity for the pastor is found in structuring retreat settings for persons in mid-life. At least once a year, congregations need to provide an outing for the medians. Middle-age adults are one of the groups in churches which seldom go for a retreat. Retreats for adults give them the chance to pull away from the pressure of life, think about their philosophy of life, discover the encouragement of others who are going through the same struggles, and develop a refreshing spirit of Christian renewal. It could be a time for informal and formal play. Medians could use the retreat as an opportunity to discover again the freedom to enjoy life and run the risk of failure. Like the church classes, retreats should focus upon a wide range of topics for discussion. Marriage enrichment is a theme which needs to be addressed often in the informal atmosphere of a retreat.

The pastoral teaching role consists not only in the pastor's personal teaching, but it must also find expression in equipping others who teach median adults. Along with preparing for their teaching experience through biblical research, Sunday School teachers should be prepared through understanding the people with whom they work. Week by week, those who teach in the median-adult age group have opportunity to discuss pertinent issues of life with their students. All through their

Bible teaching they can dispense the truth about how the gospel meets the particualr needs of people. As you teach teachers concerning mid-life, they will discover ways of making their teaching more relevant.

The teaching role of the pastor can be especially rewarding with median adults. Those adults who will submit themselves to the discipline of learning during their adult years are some of life's best learners. Adults bring a great deal of motivation, insight, and accumulated knowledge, wisdom, self-discipline, and learning skills to their classroom experiences. Too many teaching pastors play down the possibility of adults being able to learn. Much effort is directed toward the children and youth of a congregation, while adults often are overlooked. A good argument can be made for concentrating large amounts of pastoral energy in the direction of teaching adults. As adults mature and grow in their knowledge of life, they are able to influence the younger generation in a positive fashion.

Remember, as you teach, you are not the only one who is seeking to teach a generative philosophy to mid-lifers. In fact, the whole world is attempting to influence the outcome of the lives of medians. A multitude of life-style options are presented daily to adults. The philosophies offered as a way of life have to do with wealth, power, success, and pleasure. You will want to shape a generative life-style which is rooted in the good soil of loving relationship with God and man. Help adults to know how to relate the gospel of grace to loving their errant children, their struggling marriage, their social involvement in life, their responsibility as citizens to the fabric of all life, and the care and nurture of their own being.

Encourage Faith in the Midst of Crisis

The battle front for medians becomes clearly defined in the concrete crisis experiences through which they travel as persons moving toward the fulfillment of life. Most median adults do not have a clear sense of the developmental crisis which they are experiencing, but they have a vivid awareness of the day-to-day struggles which are theirs. Unless middle-age persons have chosen the road of Stoicism, one can hear them talk often concerning their children's developmental problems, their marital predicaments and joys, work and its related agenda, and the physical manifestations of their mid-life. These are some of the particular crises which are the concrete expressions of middle age. The pastor must look for the crisis events of mid-life and seek to minister to his people in their crises.

Basically, a crisis time is an occasion of distress in the life of an individual. Since persons will perceive potential stress-producing circumstances in different ways, the making of a crisis depends upon the perception of the persons who are in the midst of life's testing dilemmas. One of the pastor's keys to discovering the events which are of crisis proportion in the life of a person is in understanding the person's perception of the stress-producing event in their life. Pastors often are confused by events. Events appearing to be a crisis to the minister may only be a trivial matter to the parishioner. Likewise, the pastor's sense that an event is only a minor concern for the individual may be greatly in error. Spending time with people, listening to their evaluation of events, and noting the physical/emotional responses which they are making will aid the minister in interpreting the crisis nature of events.

1. *Move Toward the Person in Crisis.*—The pastor who hopes to share in the development of a mature philosophy of life for the median adults must meet them in the midst of their crisis experiences. It is in the midst of their crisis times that mid-lifers are asking the kinds of questions which can lead ultimately to a deeper faith. Armed with the truth of life which is being hammered out in his own life, the pastor can feel some confidence in entering into the crisis times for his adult church members. In his classic volume *The Christian Pastor,* Wayne Oates understands the pastor's ministry as one that is expressed in a primary fashion in times of crisis.[14] To be sure, there are other times in which the pastor ministers, but crises are prime times for growth in the life of an individual. The minister who seeks to share the whole of life with his people moves to the crisis time as a respected person who is trusted. When the environment of trust prevails, crisis ministry is powerful in its ability to assist persons in their growth.

Certain events seem to be predictable crises and should be so noted by those who minister. Death, sickness, hospitalization, divorce, family strife, losing or changing jobs, the departure of a child from the home, moving to a new community, and the traumatic events occurring in the lives of one's children and aging parents, all are certain to raise some level of crisis for persons going through these events. Ministers can prepare for ministry in these inevitable times of life by studying the characteristic human responses to events such as these. Preparation for caring can be made also through studying the theory and practice of ministry in each of these major crisis times of life.[15]

2. *Establish a Sense of Community and Concern.*—Not only must the minister move to encounter the person in crisis, but he must also seek to establish some sense of community with the individual. If the individual is to grow through the traumatic experience, the helper must be able to establish a sense of caring. The establishment of concern with persons is not solely dependent upon the length of time a pastor has known someone. A prior relationship of care is helpful but does not always indicate a sense of community in crisis times. Crisis seems to demand the need for a reestablishment of care. People who hurt often withdraw from any help. Hence, the task of building relationship is made more difficult. The doorway to establishing care is through patient, reflective listening. As the parishioner comes to feel the depth of another's concern, he will become more receptive to ministry. Persons simply must be allowed to tell the story of their concern, and you must listen. Listening is not the finale of the healing process, simply the overture. Through this avenue you will be serving to encourage the individuals to work through to the completion of their problems. They will sense they are not alone in their hurt. As confidence begins to rise, you will be able to challenge them to new awareness and new levels of living. It is probably best not to give too much advice in the early stages of crisis ministry. Trying to solve their problems for them might dampen their desire to become involved in discovering the way to live and doing it.

3. *The Challenge to Decide.*—Once the level of trust has been established and a person's story has been expressed, the person will need to make decisions about the present and the future. In this part of the caring process, you will be able to challenge the parishioner to make the decisions which are essential to well-being. Often, you will serve as one who confronts and challenges the person to make choices. Whether or not you use an overt manner of confrontation depends on the crisis at hand. At times, your confrontation and challenge is accomplished through the integrity of your own life and the strength of your character. Often, all you will need to do is utter the simple question, "What are you going to do about all of this?"

4. *Ongoing Support.*—As the person begins to grow in some direction of life as a result of encounter with crisis, the minister might be tempted

to believe that the crisis ministry has come to conclusion. Actually, only the initial phase has transpired. As the person works on the crisis, you will need to be available to consult and encourage. Every crisis is resolved through a process. Growth comes as human beings work all the way through their hurt and dilemma. In living out the results of one's decisions, new problems arise and the crisis may intensify and grow in complexity. The pastor must serve as one who aids the parishioner in interpreting the events which are transpiring, and in finding the encouragement of God. Phone calls, brief handwritten notes, an encouraging pat on the back, and occasional visits are powerful vehicles of continuing support. The visits can be informal counseling sessions in the minister's office or brief meetings over lunch or coffee, when appropriate. Out of this environment of consistent concern, the person finds strength to proceed in resolving the crisis and growing a philosophy of life.

5. *An Indispensable Ministry.*—Median adults need the ministry of encouragement in their crises. The development of their mature philosophy of life is something which cannot be accomplished through listening to the pastor's sermons, attending retreats, and working in the church. All of these vehicles of learning are valuable, but by themselves are incomplete. The pastor must go where the mid-life person is hurting —he must meet the individual in the midst of the particular crises of mid-life. It is in the hurt of life that median adults are most vulnerable to learn. All of the theory which they have received from their church is finally digested or rejected in the crises of their lives. When they are ill, it is an appropriate time to talk about the process of living, struggling, and dying. Unless someone meets them at the point of their grief and guilt, they will often give in to the temptation to stagnate. When they are in the midst of family conflict, they need the pastor to practice his best crisis ministry. Whatever you do, practice a ministry of encouragement with median adults.

Counseling Goals for Mid-Life Concerns

The pastor who refuses to counsel median adults who seek his help is missing a golden opportunity to fortify the faith of searching people. Like all counselees who turn to the pastor for help, mid-life persons must enter counseling with a desire to grow or the counseling process will be hampered. Those who come with such an attitude are some of the most responsive counselees a pastor will ever have the opportunity to help. Why? The middle-age person has experienced more of life, knows more of life's disappointments and pain, hopefully understands the necessity of change and adaptation, and senses the importance of time. Mid-life is one of the best times in life for counseling effectiveness.

The counseling approach will, of course, vary according to the needs of each counseling situation. Listening, asking appropriate questions, weighing the alternatives available to a person in a certain situation, reflecting feelings, offering advice and guidance, confrontation, and using Scripture and prayer, all are appropriate when used at the correct time in the counseling conversations. The counselor will discover with most median adults the necessity of using techniques that give the greatest amount of freedom to the counselee. Mid-life counselees are struggling with their life issues and often are quite resentful of helpers who seek to offer all of the answers to their life dilemmas. A heavy-handed authoritarian approach in the counseling room will possibly only delay a person's struggle with who he is and what life is all about. Don't be afraid to offer your opinion to the mid-life searcher, but don't attempt to make your interpretation the dogma of the counselee's life.

Anger, anxiety, grief, and guilt are four major themes which will continually surface in counseling the median adult. The appearance of the issues vary among persons, but if the counselor listens carefully to those he shepherds, he will hear these four themes being voiced. These are not unique concerns to the mid-life experience, as they are experienced all through life. Even so, there is a sense in which these issues find a uniquely powerful expression in the lives of median adults. Successful counseling must address these painful agendas.

1. *Anger.*—Anger must be faced. Counselees will appear on the pastor's doorstep seeking relief from this bitter pill. Many of them have been taught that anger must be suppressed. From childhood they have carried the thought that anger is unacceptable to God and the parent figures of their world. Others have been given the freedom to express their anger but not the wisdom to understand its origins. With rage, they lash out at their world. Regardless of how persons deal with anger, the result is the same if they do not come to terms with the source of it and learn to express it appropriately. Unresolved anger is the thing which kills intimacy in relationships. It causes a person to retreat from

life or to live a life of destructiveness. The pastor must seek to assist the mid-life person who is angry.

The counseling room can become a helpful place for learning to express and deal with anger. The pastoral counselor is one who helps give birth to the expression of such feelings. Once expressed, an individual is then free to investigate the origins of such strong feelings. It will do little good to tell a counselee not to be angry. The better course is to investigate the anger. The danger in counseling angry mid-life church members is they may misplace a large host of their anger on the pastor if he is unable to help them resolve their problem, or doesn't go along with their philosophy of life. The pastor will need to find strength for this ministry by dealing with his own anger in a prayerful fashion. Such personal strength will equip the minister to face another's anger and not run from it. It will allow a caring person to firmly guide the mid-life angry person toward freedom.

Anger will be one of the presenting issues in mid-life marital conflict counseling. Ministers who are not equipped practically or emotionally to deal with heavy conflict among their parishioners should seek to make healthy referrals early in the counseling contact. Mid-life families who seek the pastor's counseling assistance usually have been in conflict for a long time. The level of disintegration in the family may have already progressed to the point of separation and divorce. If so, most pastors will want to find the best help for their church families as soon as possible.[16] Pastors who are trained extensively in counseling and have the time to invest will work through the issues with their families who come in anger and conflict.

2. *Anxiety.*—Anxiety is another common theme of mid-life counseling. Median adults feel pushed to the limits of existence and turn to the resource of a caring pastor. The symptoms of their anxiety may be legion and generally are rooted in a life history marked with a general sense of poor self-worth. Life threatens the anxious on every hand. As persons attempt to fight the good fight of making sense out of life, they come to feel overwhelmed.

Helping persons with anxiety begins with accepting them as persons of value and worth. They must feel they are acceptable to God, themselves, the pastor, and all of life. The pastoral counselor will need to let them talk through their anxiety, help them discover the sources of it, assure them of God's love and acceptance, and aid them in structuring a life-style that helps to defuse their anxiety. Quite generally, the median adult can be helped with anxiety by talking through the whole concept of life and the rapid fleeting nature of earthly existence. The fear of growing old and dying may be at the root of anxiety in the middle of life. As the person learns to develop a life of prayer, worship, recreation, and intimate fellowship, his anxiety should become less of a joy-threatening event.

3. *Grief.*—Grief appears in abundance at mid-life. Much of it is anticipatory in nature. Medians are facing the loss of so much. Catch them in an open, unguarded moment, and they may open the door to the deepest thoughts of their lives and tell of their fear of dying. Listen carefully and it becomes clear they are already grieving the giving up of life. A large amount of their grief is reactionary. Friends and family members have begun to die by this time of life. Jobs have been lost, moves have been made, divorces have happened, children have left the home and turned it into an empty nest, and grief is real to the median adult.

Grief has been called the wound that heals itself. Indeed, the process of grief is well-documented.[17] Median adults, like all other human beings, have an excellent opportunity of working through every grief experience and reinvesting their energies into life. The major problem with the mid-life experience is found in the compounding of grief which comes in this season of existence. Too much grief is devastating. As a result, persons can move into a state of chronic grief and stagnate. Life becomes for these wounded persons an unending experience to be endured. The hope of joy seems lost in a sea of tears and pain. It should be noted, also, that many of those who need to experience the comfort of God are persons who are walking in grief tracks which can be traced to childhood. Pastors who counsel persons in grief will seek to help them see the multiplication of grief which is taking place at the midpoint of their lives. Such knowledge is helpful to grievers. Allowing them to verbalize the many attendant feelings such as anger, fear, and depression will allow the healing of grief to progress. The pastoral counselor seeks to aid the expression of the pain, not to suppress the pain. Grief counseling is a process which pastors must know thoroughly.[18]

4. *Guilt.*—Guilt quite often runs deep at the mid-point of life. The power to generate a productive life is being defused in many median

adults by the stinging reality of guilt. As the pastor traces the guilt to its source, he discovers that it is both appropriate and inappropriate guilt. It is important to distinguish between the two sources and aid the sufferer in discovering the degree of appropriateness to his guilt. Some are carrying an abundance of condemnation born of a heritage which communicated the person's unworthiness. Others are fighting to suppress the feelings of guilt which stem from occasions when they transgressed the right way of life.

As the pastor listens to the tales of mid-life, he will aid persons to come to terms with their guilt. Through confession, prayer, receiving forgiveness, and determining to live a life of repentance and (in some instances) restitution, the mid-life individual can begin to sing the song of salvation's joy. Take care not to assign all guilt to some real source of sin. Help the person learn how to diagnose the source of guilt and how to receive the grace of God in Jesus Christ. Once the guilt is relieved, there is freedom to invest more energy into the way of faith and generativity.

Conclusion

Of his own mid-life journey, Howard Clinebell wrote: "From a perspective halfway through the years from forty to sixty-five, I can say that the mid-years to date have been the most fulfilling and productive period of my life. They also have been a time of painful problems and accelerating losses."[19] Such is the reality of life in the middle. Painful, yes. Hopefully, it is the most fulfilling and productive time of life that people will live. It can be just that if persons are able to develop a mature philosophy of life that makes sense out of all the problems, pains, and losses. The church of Jesus Christ has a lot to say about the possibility of developing such a good life. Through teaching, encouraging, and counseling, ministers who care can help the middle-adult experience to be a time of growth and an opportunity for deepening one's faith . . . on the go!

Notes

1. Daniel J. Levinson, et. al., *The Seasons of a Man's Life* (New York:

Ballantine Books, 1978); Gail Sheehy, *Passages: Predictable Crises of Adult Life* (New York: Bantam Books, 1977).

2. Lewis Joseph Sherrill, *The Struggle of the Soul* (New York: Macmillan Publishing Co., Inc., 1951), p. 150.

3. Levinson, p. 60.

4. Gail Sheehy, p. 364.

5. Ibid., p. 350.

6. Warren W. Wiersbe, "Mid-life Crises? Bah, Humbug!" *Christianity Today* (May 21, 1982), p. 26.

7. Gail Sheehy, p. 356.

8. Howard J. Clinebell, Jr., *Growth Counseling for Mid-Years Couples* (Philadelphia: Fortress Press, 1977), p. 22.

9. Gail Sheehy, *The Pathfinders* (New York: William Morrow and Co., Inc., 1981).

10. See Cecil R. Paul, *Passages of a Pastor* (Grand Rapids: Zondervan Publishing House, 1981) and Louis McBurney, *Every Pastor Needs a Pastor* (Waco: Word Books, 1977), for excellent help in coming to terms with the stresses and personal needs of the pastor.

11. Wayne E. Oates, *The Christian Pastor,* 3rd ed., revised (Philadelphia: The Westminster Press, 1982), pp. 89-91.

12. See John Claypool, *Stages: The Art of Living the Expected* (Waco: Word Books, 1977) for a sample series of sermons on the developmental stages of life.

13. Reuel Howe, *The Creative Years* (New York: Seabury Press, 1959) and William E. Hulme, *Mid-Life Crises* (Philadelphia: The Westminster Press, 1980).

14. Wayne E. Oates, pp. 17-64.

15. See C. W. Brister, *Pastoral Care in the Church* (New York: Harper and Row, Publishers, 1964), pp. 167-256, and Marcus D. Bryant, *The Art of Christian Caring* (St. Louis: The Bethany Press, 1979) for helpful summaries on caring during the crisis moments of existence.

16. Helpful clues on making positive referrals are found in William B. Oglesby's *Referral in Pastoral Counseling* (Philadelphia: Fortress Press, 1968) and Wayne E. Oates and Kirk H. Neely's *Where to Go for Help,* rev. and enlarged ed. (Philadelphia: The Westminster Press, 1972).

17. See Robert W. Bailey, *The Minister and Grief* (New York: Hawthorn Books, 1976) for a summary descriptive analysis of grief and the pastor's role in grief work.

18. An invaluable volume for understanding the process of counseling with those who grieve is Wayne E. Oates' *Pastoral Care and Counseling in Grief and Separation* (Philadelphia: Fortress Press, 1976).

19. Clinebell, p. 1.

Additional Bibliography

Brister, C. W. *The Promise of Counseling.* San Francisco: Harper and Row, Publishers, 1978.

Coleman, Lucien E., Jr. *Understanding Adults.* Nashville: Convention Press, 1969.

Gleason, John J., Jr. *Growing Up to God: Eight Steps in Religious Development.* Nashville: Abingdon Press, 1975.

Hulme, William E. *Mid-Life Crises.* Philadelphia: The Westminster Press, 1980.

Paul, Cecil R. *Passages of a Pastor.* Grand Rapids, Michigan: Zondervan Publishing House, 1981.

Stagg, Frank. *The Bible Speaks on Aging.* Nashville: Broadman Press, 1981.

Tournier, Paul. *The Seasons of Life.* Translated by John S. Gilmour. Richmond, Virginia: John Knox Press, 1973.

6
Senior Adulthood: Twilight or Dawn?
Albert L. Meiburg

Two of my senior friends have retired recently. I have been interested in their experiences, not only because they are friends whom I respect, but also because I need to plan for my own later years. They have been my unwitting teachers, as from the sidelines I watched them grappling with the issues of later adulthood. I am grateful to each of them for prompting me to think more seriously about the years ahead.

Harold seemed oblivious to his approaching retirement. So far as I could tell, he was expecting to continue his business indefinitely into the future. There were several points, however, which it seemed to me he was overlooking. He had a number of vague physical symptoms that eluded the doctor. He looked chronically tired. He complained about not being able to remember his customer's names as well as he had in the past. Small frustrations, such as getting a parking ticket, became major issues.

Harold seemed stuck in a rut. On one hand, his complaints suggested he was under stress. On the other hand, he seemed unwilling to take the signs of stress seriously enough to do something about them. For example, he turned down several opportunities to make business arrangements which would have given him some income while allowing him to reduce his daily work load. His reluctance to make any changes in his life said to me that he was afraid of the future.

The future can be scarey at any age. Teen-agers, while often excited by the prospect of adult privileges, are at the same time frightened by adult responsibilities. Some senior adults, like Harold, equate aging with decline. They see it as a threat to their present way of life and fear anticipated losses. For them, the guiding image of aging seems to be that of the close of day: *twilight*. Can you blame them for not wanting to rush toward the sunset?

Murray's approach to retirement was about as different from Harold's as night is from day. On several occasions he discussed with me various options he had under consideration. Twenty years before he reached retirement age, he bought a piece of worn-out farmland and planted it in fast-growing trees.

About a year before he had planned to retire, an old illness flared up, and I wondered if he would move the date up. Little chance! He stuck with his doctors but kept up a reduced work schedule. Gradually his symptoms subsided.

Murray seemed to take a peculiar delight in the formal celebration of his retirement. He invited a number of old friends. He reminisced about the struggles of his earlier years, took a lot of good-natured ribbing about his peculiarities, and shared some of his plans for the future. A firm in a nearby city had invited him to do some consulting. He was considering running for town council.

Murray was aware of some of the hazards of old age, but he did not dwell on them. His response was to take the initiative. He began planning for retirement early. As I watched him enter a new phase of his life, the image which seemed to guide him was that of a new day: *dawn*. He seemed to be moving forward with hope.

Why such different perspectives on the common experience of aging? This is not a simple question to answer, because people aren't simple. To begin with, each person is born with a unique genetic make-up, except for identical twins. Again, with few exceptions, each child in the family has a unique birth order. Throughout life there is an infinite variety of experiences which leave a deposit in the life of the individual. Thus, the longer they live, the more diverse people tend to become. Senior adults are not stamped out with a cookie cutter!

Older people tend to deal with the issues of their aging pretty much like they have dealt with life issues in preceeding stages. Some, like Harold, fear the dark. Others, like Murray, believe with Zechariah that "at evening time it shall be light."[1] However, these are not the only alternatives. There is a continuum of perspectives, of which twilight and dawn symbolize the polarities.

Can we generalize about older people, given their uniqueness and individuality? While we must always be cautious in applying the general characteristics of a group to any one individual, we can identify some issues which are fairly common in later life. As we have seen, people may respond to them quite differently, but an understanding of the developmental tasks which face older people can alert us to their needs.

The Developmental Tasks of Senior Adulthood

For many years the literature of human development focused almost exclusively on childhood and adolescence, with little attention to adulthood and none to aging. The example of the pioneer American psychologist G. Stanley Hall, who wrote significant early works on both adolescence *and* senescence (aging), was not followed by his successors.

Happily the situation is changing. The appearance within recent years of both scholarly and popular works on adult development illustrates the growing attention being given to the psychology of maturity.

Early studies of aging by behavioral scientists arose from concern with the unmet needs of the elderly, according to Neugarten.[2] This led to a problem-centered view, not unlike the way in which Freud's practice with neurotics influenced the perspective of psychoanalysis. However, as research findings began to multiply and more representative samples of older people were studied, the great diversity of the patterns of successful aging became apparent.

The Concept of Developmental Tasks

During the 1930s and early 1940s, educators were interested in discovering the best time for learning various skills, such as reading. They found a parallel between the concept of the "critical period" in the development of the embryo and the readiness of individuals to undertake certain learning tasks.

In the 1930s the growth of young people was often compared with that of a plant, which, given proper supplies of nutrients, light, and water, would develop and bear fruit. The person's own responsibility for his development was not emphasized.

A more sophisticated model of development emerged in the concept of the "developmental task." According to Robert J. Havighurst, one of its best-known proponents, developmental tasks arise from three sources: physical maturation, cultural pressures, and the aspirations and values of the individual. In his classic definition of the "teachable moment," Havighurst incorporates all three sources: "When the body is ripe, and society requires, and the self is ready to achieve a certain task, the teachable moment has come."[3]

Developmental Tasks in Later Maturity

If children grow mentally, emotionally, and socially in a predictable sequence, reasoned some behavioral scientists, why shouldn't adults do likewise? What began as the field of "child development" was broadened to "human development." Several authorities have attempted to identify the developmental tasks of later life. What follows is a brief summary of some of their findings.

Havighurst was among the earliest to spell out the growth issues in middle age and later maturity. Here are the tasks he suggested as central to late life.[4]

1. Adjusting to decreasing physical strength and health
2. Adjusting to retirement and reduced income
3. Adjusting to the death of one's spouse
4. Establishing an affiliation with one's age group
5. Maintaining civic and social obligations
6. Establishing satisfactory housing arrangements

Evelyn M. Duvall, who studied with Havighurst at Chicago, applied the developmental task concept to families. She developed a text in family life education which showed how the family has a life cycle of its own, and how the tasks of family members interact. Her list of the tasks of older couples include some but not all of Havighurst's items. She added some tasks not given by Havighurst.[5]

1. Finding a satisfying home for the later years
2. Adjusting to retirement income
3. Establishing comfortable household routines
4. Nurturing each other as husband and wife
5. Facing bereavement and widowhood
6. Maintaining contact with children and grandchildren
7. Caring for elderly relatives
8. Keeping an interest in people outside the family
9. Finding meanings in life

Erik H. Erikson, like Havighurst, envisioned a lifelong scheme of developmental challenges. However, instead of a "list" of tasks, he sought to define one main task for each life-stage. If one has not "done his homework" for a particular stage, he may continue to work on it in the next stage although this results in complications. The tasks are stated in terms of opposing tendencies.

Erikson considers the essential task of late life to be the achievement of ego-integrity versus a sense of despair.[6] By "integrity" he means a basic acceptance of one's life as having been inevitable, appropriate, and meaningful.

Failure to accomplish this task is responsible for the fear of death (despair), the feeling that time has run out, that there is no chance to start life over. On the other hand, the achievement of integrity produces the "virtue" of wisdom, which Erikson defines as "the detached and yet active concern with life itself in the face of death itself."[7]

There is an important connection, in Erikson's thought, between the eighth and final stage of growth and the key task of the preceding stage (mid-life): generativity versus stagnation. As he puts it, "Only in him who in some way has taken care of things and people and has adapted himself to the triumphs and disappointments adherent to being the originator of others or the generator of products and ideas—only in him may gradually ripen the fruit of these seven stages. I know of no better word for it than integrity."[8]

Robert C. Peck noted that Erikson's eighth stage summed up all the psychological crises of the last forty to fifty years of life. Following Erikson's pattern of opposing tendencies, he proposed to further define three tasks for old age.[9]

1. Ego differentiation versus work-role preoccupation. When the last child leaves home, parents have to find a replacement for parenting as a basis for selfhood. Similarly, retirement requires individuals to define themselves in ways other than their traditional work-roles.

2. Body transcendance versus body preoccupation. In the course of normal aging, all of us will face some sort of physical limits. Peck asks whether we will allow the physical changes associated with aging to dominate our lives, or whether we can still find challenge and satisfaction in creative mental activities and human relationships.

3. Ego transcendence versus ego preoccupation. Old age brings with it the certain prospect of personal death. The choice, as Peck sees it, is between passive resignation to the inevitable on one hand and a deep, active effort to make life better for those who come after, on the other.

The following table gives a simplified overview of the perspectives of the authorities cited above. While terms may vary, there is a considerable amount of agreement. Something of a consensus emerges. Three

Developmental Tasks of Late Life
According to Various Authorities

TASKS	HAVIGHURST	DUVALL	ERIKSON	PECK
1. Adjusting to decreasing physical health and strength	X			X
2. Adjusting to retirement and reduced income	X	X		X
3. Adjusting to death of spouse	X	X		
4. Affiliating with one's age group	X			
5. Meeting social and civic responsibilities	X	X		
6. Establishing satisfactory housing arrangements	X	X		
7. Finding meanings in life in the face of death		X	X	X
8. Nurturing one another as husband and wife		X		
9. Maintaining contact with children and grandchildren		X		
10. Caring for elderly relatives		X		

of the four sources identify the issues of health status, retirement, and meaning in life as key tasks.

Developmental Tasks and Pastoral Care

What is the relevance of these developmental tasks for pastoral care? The developmental perspective informs and enhances pastoral care in three ways: (1) it broadens our understanding of the aging process; (2) it identifies specific growth needs of individuals; (3) it suggests a central focus for the caring process.

One way a developmental perspective informs pastoral care is by disclosing the many faces of aging. Too often we see the last stage of life in only one dimension—the dimension of physical decline. An ancient example of this face of aging is given by the "philosopher" of Ecclesiastes in these words:

Then your arms, that have protected you will tremble, and your legs, now strong, will grow weak. Your teeth will be too few to chew your food, and your eyes too dim to see clearly. Your ears will be deaf to the noise of the street. You will barely be able to hear the mill as it grinds or music as it plays, but even the song of a bird will wake you from sleep.

You will be afraid of high places, and walking will be dangerous. Your hair will turn white; you will hardly be able to drag yourself along, and all desire will be gone (12:3-5a).[10]

The spectrum of developmental tasks makes it clear that coping with inevitable physical limitations is by no means the only challenge of later life. It may be the most obvious, but that doesn't make it the most important. Notice that of the ten tasks listed in the table, at least six (numbers 3,4,5,8,9,10) require one to relate to other persons in some way. The social matrix of aging is obviously important.

A second way in which a developmental approach supports pastoral care is by providing a diagnostic framework. A review of the common developmental tasks can indicate the specific growing edges of a particular person at a particular time. Caring can then proceed with a clear sense of direction.

A third way in which developmental understanding enhances pastoral care is by suggesting a central focus for the caring process. For example, if we follow Erikson's scheme, we take the primary goal of our care to be encouraging the person in the pursuit of meaning (ego-integrity). This means supporting persons as they come to terms with their limits, as they celebrate the joy and wisdom they have garnered, and as they discover ways to keep on living and growing.

Offering pastoral care is like taking a journey along with a fellow human being. We don't need previous personal experience of every turn in the road to know where we are headed. We can have both the confidence of a known direction and the excitement of wonderful surprises along the way.

Erikson reminds us that aging is a spiritual experience. It is spiritual in terms of the issues at stake and their potential significance for the individual. Old age is our last chance in this life to become the person God intended us to be.

The spirituality of aging is not a mystical gift that arrives along with a Medicare card on one's sixty-fifth birthday. Certainly not all senior adults take an explicitly religious view of life. Surveys of the religious interest of older people, or of their participation in religious activities (e.g., church attendance) are not convincing proofs of the intrinsic spirituality of aging.

However, aging does bring with it the potential of spiritual growth.

Whether or not this potential is realized depends upon several factors. One such factor is the life-style and value system of the individual. Some persons will intuitively seek continuity between their personal heritage and the present situation and draw on their faith as a resource. Others may remain as oblivious to the spiritual dimensions of life as they always have been.

Effective pastoral care may be another factor which determines whether the growth potential of aging is actualized for a given person. In fact, the aim of pastoral care is to challenge senior adults to discover the growth possibilities before them and to sustain and encourage them through the resources of their faith. The remainder of the chapter explores this process of caring.

Pastoral Care with Senior Adults

How can pastoral care be offered effectively with senior adults in the light of developmental perspectives? That is the question to be explored. The discussion which follows gives attention both to pastoral care practice and to the assumptions which can guide and correct it.

Guiding Assumptions

We bring to any ministry certain assumptions about the task, about those it involves, and about ourselves. Therefore, before proceeding to actual practice, we should try to put into words certain principles which make for effectiveness.

1. *Caregivers must come to terms with their own aging.*—For pastoral care to be effective, the agent, pastor or lay caregiver, must be emotionally available to the person being cared for. In the context of senior adulthood, this means that caregivers must have taken a deliberate look at their feelings about their own aging. To neglect this is to risk superficiality.

For example, some authorities suggest that the fear of death is virtually universal, and that we tend to cope with it by various mental strategies of which denial is the chief.[11] Therefore, because older people remind us of the ultimate end of our own lives, we may be inclined toward a pattern of avoidance.

We can avoid the threat of aging in two directions. On one hand we can idealize aging, emphasizing its rewards and blessings, but ignoring its pain and struggle. This often results in a superficial approach to ministry in which major attention is given to activity for its own sake, and people are not encouraged to explore their deeper concerns.

On the other hand, we can "demonize" aging, by seeing only its sufferings and by disregarding its growth possibilities. Our fears may then cause us to avoid involvement with senior adults. In either case, senior adults are not well served.

The significance of one's own feelings about aging for pastoral care was illustrated for me when Wallace, a seminary student with a special interest in pastoral care, showed up in my course, "Ministry with Older Persons." Wallace shared with me that he had enrolled in the course because of his fear of older people. He traced this to his childhood when a grandparent living in his home made life miserable for him and his parents.

With my encouragement, Wallace became a volunteer chaplain in a nursing home. As he began to acknowledge his reluctance to relate to older people his attitude began to change. He developed an interest in a long-mute resident of the home. One day, while he visited with her, she opened her eyes and spoke to him! This was a turning point. After completing seminary, he decided to prepare for a full-time career in senior adult ministry.

2. *Caring "with" is better than caring "for."*—A preposition is a small word, but sometimes it can make a big difference in meaning. Caring "for" implies that the recipient of care is to some extent dependent. By contrast, caring "with" connotes a sense of comradeship and mutuality.

The concept of caring "with" emphasizes the importance of seeing senior adults as capable of self-direction, decision making, and caring for others. When we care "with," we support autonomy and dignity.

The notion of caring "for" may unwittingly confirm the low self-image of some senior adults. There is an assumption by some that when they reach sixty-five, people should withdraw "active life" and let younger people "take over." When we care "for," we may encourage passivity and noninvolvement.

A good indication of whether we are caring "with" or caring "for" older people is the degree to which senior adults are participants in the planning and execution of the church's ministries with senior adults.[12]

Seeking the wisdom of the older members of the church in program planning says to them that they are still needed.

3. *Caring with seniors must address the whole family.*—Janet had looked forward to retirement for some time. After a busy career she was hoping for the freedom to travel, visit friends, and enjoy a more leisurely pace. Janet's mother had looked forward to Janet's retirement also, but for different reasons. She had lived on by herself in the rambling farmhouse since her husband died years before, but now she was too feeble to continue without assistance.

In the face of her mother's needs, Janet felt she had no choice but to defer her own plans. She sold her house in the city and moved back "home." Her mother expected Janet's total attention. To her pastor, Janet confessed, "I love Mother, but I am frustrated, angry, and depressed. If I try to make the farm *my* home, Mother objects, yet she insists I must be there all the time!"

Here we have a real-life example of the importance of the assumption, that in caring for seniors, we must address the family, and not just the older person in isolation. In this situation, the needs of the "young old" daughter are in conflict with those of her "old old" mother. Pastoral care must take into account the needs of both.

Janet's dilemma is an increasingly common concern of younger senior adults today: how to maintain their own life and health while sustaining their aging parents. Several facts underscore the importance of family issues for informed caring.

Most older people have families who care for them and with whom they are in fairly frequent communication. The myth that most older people are neglected by their children has been shown by a number of studies not to be so.[13]

Other older people are without children and need a substitute. Emotional support can be provided by friends, extended kin, and by the church.

The role of caregiver to aging parents is most often assigned to women. In a day when 60 percent of American women are employed outside the home, many feel severely burdened by this since they may still have adolescent children at home as well. Effective caring must be sensitive to the impact of aging on the whole family structure.

4. *Caring includes mobilizing the available resources.*—Arnold had been

a widower for twelve years before developing an incurable brain disease. He had no children, but Arnold's friends at work rallied around him. At first, while his limitations were mild, they kept him included in things, by driving him to work, and by assigning him routine tasks he could still do.

There came a time, however, when it was necessary for him to retire because of his disability. Even then, his friends stood by him. One came by weekly to help him pay his bills. Another took him out for a meal occasionally. A third took him along when he went to the barber shop.

For almost a year, Arnold was enabled to remain in his own home because of the heroic efforts of his "family," along with such community support as Meals-on-Wheels, and a paid companion. Arnold's needs were so diverse and so great that no single person or agency alone could have met them. Caring for Arnold required a team effort.

Caring for senior adults is usually more effective when it is approached as a team effort rather than single-handedly. If you feel overwhelmed by the needs of a senior adult, consider enlisting the aid of others: family, friends, or community agency. For assistance in discovering the resources in your community, contact your county Council on Aging.

As we turn now to the practice of pastoral care, we will find occasions to refer to these guiding assumptions.

The Practice of Pastoral Care

Senior adulthood can extend for thirty or more years, making it one of the longer periods in the life span. Just as we understand the needs of teenagers as being different from those of toddlers, so also, we understand that within the senior years there is a diversity of needs. Gerontologists are suggesting that the life needs of persons newly retired differ markedly from those in their eighties and beyond.[14] In keeping with the general scheme of this book, then, we will look first at pastoral care with the newly old.

1. *Enablement and Challenge: Caring with "Young" Seniors.*—The major themes of pastoral care with "young" seniors are enablement and challenge. By "enablement," I mean the pastor's efforts in opening doors for their continued participation both in church and community.

By "challenge," I mean the pastor's efforts to stimulate the personal growth and development of persons.

Retirement from the work force is one of the most significant yet ambiguous passages in the life cycle. Many Americans look forward to it as a reward for a lifetime of hard work. At the same time, they may dread its connotation of being "put on the shelf."

We have no rite of passage except for the "retirement dinner" and we don't even have that for women whose careers are those of mother and homemaker. John Westerhoff and William Willimon have offered thoughtful suggestions for a worship service to acknowledge retirement.[15] Such a service would seek to interpret this event in the light of the gospel, to affirm the continuing personhood of those retiring, and to dramatize the challenges and opportunities of their new life. However, until the church has led people to approach the significant changes in their lives from the perspective of faith, simply holding recognition services is not likely to be very meaningful.

When the individual has some say so about the actual beginning of retirement, has some sort of financial security, and is in reasonably good health, the prospect is likely to be one of a welcomed sense of freedom.

Affirming this freedom, and exploring its meaning for the about-to-be and the newly retired, is an appropriate form of enablement in this phase of aging. Take Vivian, for example.

A widow with no children, Vivian had been very happy in her career with a national company. Her husband had owned his own business. After he died, she continued her own work, remained in their home, and enjoyed her church friends. However, when she became eligible for early retirement, she decided to move back to her home state to be near her brothers and sisters.

For Vivian, the retirement which she chose seems to be going well. She bought a nice condominium, with some new furnishings. Her health is good. She keeps in touch with her family, makes occasional trips by car to visit out-of-state friends, and does volunteer work. Vivian is typical of today's new generation of energetic "young old" folks who are confident, useful, and happy.

Pastoral care with Vivian would include affirming her freedom and exploring her goals for retirement. The pastor in the community to which she retired could help her discover ways in which her talents and interests could be useful to the church and community. He could introduce her to those in the church who would include her in activities. She might be enlisted as a member of the senior adult council to aid in planning a balanced program of Bible study, educational, recreational, and outreach ministries as Horace Kerr has suggested.[16]

Senior adults in certain professions are able to manage their retirements as a process rather than as an event. They work out a gradual reduction in demands at a pace with which they are comfortable. This gives them both a desired sense of freedom and the satisfaction of work they enjoy.

More older people would like to continue some sort of employment than are able to at the present time.[17] In this respect, Alice has been very fortunate.

She was the oldest of six children and grew up on a farm. Her father, an industrious man who lived to be 84, wanted Alice to be a teacher and helped her go to college. She began teaching but gave it up when she married, to work in her husband's business.

At 40 years of age, Alice unexpectedly became pregnant. She and her husband had always wanted children but had been told by their physician that they could not have any. Alice "retired" to become a full-time mother to a beautiful baby girl. This, her third "career," lasted fifteen years.

When her daughter was well-along in high school, Alice bought a small shop which she enjoyed running until her husband died. This was a hard blow. She sold the shop and took a while to think about her future.

Then, at a time when most people retire, Alice found a job as a weekend relief telephone operator at a nearby hospital. Now 78, her "retirement job" puts Alice in touch with people, gives her the satisfaction of serving her community, and yet its demands are not burdensome.

The freedom and meaning in retirement which Vivian and Alice have found are by no means universal. If the decision to retire is imposed by illness or employer policy, it may be unwelcome. Feelings of bitterness or helplessness may result. When this is the case, pastoral care can enable the person to explore alternatives and experiment with a new life-style.

Even when retirement is welcomed, there may be some unanticipated complications. The pastor should not underestimate the significance of the shift from employment to retirement. Well-intentioned friends, and even retirees themselves, may fail to appreciate the impact of the changes which retirement brings.

"Retirement shock" may result from the sense of loss in a person who has strong ties to his or her work and has found in it a sense of meaning and identity. Harried middle-aged or younger friends, whose image of retirement is that of an unending vacation, are likely to envy their retired friend's independence from schedules and deadlines. They may, therefore, overlook the mixed feelings of the retiree, expressing their assumptions in such remarks as "Now that you have so much time on your hands, how about helping me with this volunteer work?" or, "Well, I'll bet you are really enjoying having time to catch up on your golf, now that you are your own boss!"

The pervasive changes which retirement or relocation brings are graphically described by Sarah-Patton Boyle in a recent autobiographical account titled *The Desert Blooms*.[18] Eagerly, and somewhat naively, she sought to make a new beginning in retirement. She had enjoyed homemaking, but after her husband left and her children were grown, she decided to move from a college town to the suburbs of Washington, D.C., to begin a new life.

She was not prepared for the shock which awaited her. At first, she was busy decorating her apartment to her own taste and exploring the shopping centers, art galleries, parks, and churches. She felt like a jack-in-the-box suddenly released.[19]

Within a few months, however, she made a painful discovery: "My luxurious sense of freedom to do what I choose when I choose was gone! Far from plunging into painting and writing, as I had expected, I felt immobilized."[20] The demands of outside pressures from which she had previously escaped through her writing were no longer there, but she faced a new bondage: "the weight of petty decisions."

It was natural for Patty Boyle to turn to her church in this crisis. She had been a life-long Christian. She did, in fact, find friends in the church fellowship, including the pastor and his wife. But despite the helpfulness of many in the church, she found that even there the pain of her personal struggle was only dimly perceived. Her experience shows clearly that we cannot assume that retirement is pure joy. There may be joys in it, but there is also hard work.

For folks like Patty Boyle, the pastoral task lies in affirming the freedom of the retiree, while remaining alert to the possibility of retirement shock. If her pastor had realized how helpless Patty felt, he might have intervened more effectively in her struggle to build a new life. Challenging the "young old" to find new ways to care for the world, the community, and other persons will forestall stagnation, loneliness, and self-pity.

2. *Advocacy and Support: Caring with Frail Seniors.*—Of all people over 65, only about 20 per cent report having to limit their activities because of impaired health.[21] However, at some point in the aging process, health problems are likely to create concern. When they are severe enough to threaten continued independent living, pastoral advocacy and support are called for.

It is not unusual for older people to allude to their health concerns during pastoral calls. Such concerns should be taken seriously. If the person has not had medical attention recently, he or she may be encouraged to consult the family doctor. The studies mentioned above suggest that the pastor should be alert to a discrepancy between the health assessment of older people themselves and that of their physicians. Some people minimize serious problems, while others dramatize minor ones. The pastor may want to ask the person's permission to confer with his doctor, or he may make a referral to a comprehensive geriatric evaluation clinic for assessment and recommendation. The latter service, usually available in major medical centers, can be helpful in dealing with more complex or puzzling health-related problems.

Ellen and Howard's story illustrates the theme of pastoral advocacy and support. When Howard was 58, anticipating retirement, they bought several acres of land on the outskirts of town and built a house, doing much of the work themselves. It was to be their last move. For twenty years they were very happy there.

Then, two years ago, Howard had a stroke. He is mentally alert, but limited in mobility. He gets about some by using a walker. Ellen, at 74, continues in good health, and takes good care of Howard. However, she does not drive, and so now both of them are pretty much confined at home.

Both their children are married. Their daughter lives about five hours away, and their son, a career Navy officer, is stationed in California.

For many years they were active members of their church. Ellen sang in the choir. Howard was a deacon and Sunday School teacher. Since Howard's stroke they can no longer attend. However, they have kept up all the ties they can. They send their offering, and they welcome visitors from the church.

Now, in addition to Howard's stroke, a new turn of events has occurred which threatens Ellen and Howard. A developer acquired all the land surrounding their property and plans to build a shopping center. He offered a generous price for their place. The pastor made a call as soon as he heard the news. He listened as they shared their feelings.

Ellen, looking out the window at her garden, said, "I put out three new roses last year. When the dry weather came, I saved dish water and took it out to keep them alive . . . but now, well . . . it's all gone."

Howard, his eyes filling with tears, said, "I feel like I'm losing everything I've worked for all these years. We have loved this place and thought we'd be right here until we died. I can't do much myself anymore, but I can enjoy what we did together . . . and our neighbors, how can we leave them? I just don't feel like starting over at my age!"

How can pastoral advocacy and support be given to Howard and Ellen? Many possibilities come to mind. They can be summarized in three points: (1) provide continuity in a time of tumultuous change, (2) mobilize a support system for extending independence, and (3) share in the task of life-review.

The immediate crisis is one of grief as this couple anticipates the loss of their home, and with it a cherished identity and way of life. The pastor's first instinct, to listen, will help them to grieve. Listening is supportive.

Howard and Ellen can't just grieve, however. They have to move, but the question is *where?* The pastor can help them explore alternatives for the next chapter in their lives. Should they stay in this community, or move nearer one of their children? Should they consider entering a retirement community which offers the possibility of lifetime care, if Howard's condition should change?

More is involved in the consideration of moving than simply a choice among housing options. Howard and Ellen want to find a place where they can continue as many as possible of those pursuits which have given their lives meaning and purpose. The pastor helps them rank the options in terms of their lifelong values, and may serve as an advocate for their right to make decisions for themselves.

During this time of tumultuous change for Howard and Ellen, the pastor can provide a point of continuity between their cherished past and an uncertain future. Their faith is a resource for them, as it was for Patty Boyle.

In her essay referred to earlier in this chapter, Sarah-Patton Boyle described the gulf between life as she had known it and her new life. She felt a deep need for "one area of stability, one unaltered link" with her past: "In the bewildering brokenness of my patterns of living, the church alone stood steady and unaltered, reaching back into my earliest childhood—a visible, touchable, long-remembered expression of my faith and a steadfast symbol of the unchanging love of God."[2] The pastor symbolizes that faith and that love, and tries to incarnate it in relationships with the frail elderly.

In this enterprise, the pastor is not alone. In addition to personal caring, the pastor can help to mobilize an appropriate support system for helping the frail elderly to maintain independent living for as long as possible. (Refer to the guiding assumptions noted earlier concerning family involvement and mobilizing the available resources, especially the case of Arnold.)

For Howard and Ellen, a support system might entail several elements. Their children would need to be considered. They might welcome sensitive guidance as to how they can best be supportive of their parents while still respecting their dignity and autonomy. Various components of the church, such as the homebound program of the Sunday school or tape ministry, might be appropriate. Depending upon the sort of location Howard and Ellen choose, community services could be utilized. The main point here is that the pastor continues his personal support while at the same time seeing that the resources of family, church, and community are coordinated.

Another avenue of support available to the pastor in the care of Howard and Ellen is sharing in the task of life-review. Some years ago,

Dr. Robert Butler called attention to this phenomenon which has received considerable attention in the literature of gerontology.[23] Dr. Butler pointed out that reminiscence, often viewed negatively as "living in the past," could serve a constructive purpose for older people, if they had a sensitive partner. Life-review is a developmental task faced not only by older people but by those of any age who anticipate death. It is an effort to separate the grain of life from its chaff. The pastor, or a trusted friend who is a good listener, can become a partner in this adventure in meaning.

The clue to the possible utility of life-review in the case of Howard and Ellen lies in Howard's feeling of helplessness. Ellen seemed a bit more flexible as she faced this transition. At one point she said to the pastor, "It's funny how things work out—seems to prepare you over the years for what's next." Although she shared Howard's grief, Ellen seemed to have some hope.

Howard, by contrast, found it difficult to deal with relocating. He did not feel able to "start all over again," so he saw no future for himself. Having planned to die here, it is almost as if when he has to leave, his life is over. Life-review may be a way of helping Howard to get in touch with his essential identity, which has roots much further back in his life than his ownership of this particular piece of real-estate.

The physical task of moving will evoke many memories. Howard and Ellen will have to separate the keepsakes and heirlooms from the junk they have collected. In the process, they may gain a new perspective on their life story if they have the attention of an empathic listener. The listener's role is to look for continuity, for patterns, and above all for enduring meanings. To lift these up, to affirm them, and to understand the associated feelings is a rewarding pastoral experience, and could help Howard find new purpose in his remaining years.

Life-review may take various forms. Writing or taping autobiographies is perhaps the most obvious. Another idea might be to make a scrapbook of old photographs and clippings for one's children. Sometimes suggesting that a younger family member take a life history of a grandparent can result in important family communication.

Whatever its form, the goal of the life-review is what Erikson described as the central developmental task of aging, the achievement of a sense of integrity, of "rightness" about one's life, rather than a sense of despair and defeat.

Ultimately, life-review should free one to deal with the present. An Old Testament illustration comes from Isaiah. His encouragement to Israel in Babylon begins with a reminder of God's help at the Red Sea, when they were trying to escape an earlier captivity:

Long ago the Lord made a road through the sea, a path through the swirling waters. . . .
But the Lord says,
"Do not cling to events of the past
   or dwell on what happened long ago.
Watch for the new thing I am going to do.
   It is happening already—you can see it now!
I will make a road through the wilderness
   and give you streams of water there."[24]

Howard's reflection should help him to "watch for the new thing" that the Lord may be doing in his life.

"Good memories can be refreshing," notes Patty Boyle, "and bad ones can be learned from. But, good or bad, when memories hamper present functioning, it is time turn them out."[25]

As we have seen, most "younger" senior adults and many of the "frail elderly" are relatively well and active. However, no treatment of pastoral care with senior adults would be complete without recognizing the needs of those who are coping with physical and mental impairments. We turn now to this concern.

2. Respect and Closeness: Caring with Impaired Seniors.—Sometimes health problems of later life leave senior adults with degrees of impairment. The central themes in caring with impaired seniors are respect and closeness. The isolation which can result from physical, sensory, or mental impairment calls for pastoral initiative in bridging the barriers to communication and in supporting personal dignity.

Familiar examples of physical handicap with which older people have to cope are the gradual loss of mobility from arthritis and the sudden paralysis from a stroke. The loss of mastery and the sense of having to depend on others to meet personal needs can seriously damage a person's dignity.

If the impairment also results in disfigurement, as sometimes happens in the facial paralysis following stroke, a person may feel shame. Embarrassment may be felt by older people who become incontinent but are mentally alert. Any of these impairments may damage a person's confidence to the point that he or she may be tempted to withdraw.

Caregivers with handicapped seniors can do much to offset withdrawal if they convey a genuine respect which takes into account the total person, not just the visible impairment. Pastors, friends, and family, knowing the person's history, can emphasize his or her uniqueness.

We show respect when we affirm a person's right to privacy and to decision making. These elements are more difficult to realize in the setting of institutional care than in a person's own home. A space of one's own, a space for one's "stuff," including significant memorabilia, is a tangible expression of respect.

Since impairments reduce the amount of control persons have over so much of their lives, whatever can be done to respect their wishes and to give them choices is helpful. I remember with gratitude when this happened to my sister. She had just entered the nursing home. She wanted to be cooperative, but for some reason she didn't enjoy the worship service on Sunday afternoon. It was a relief and a reassurance to her when the director of the home said to her, "If you don't want to go, just stay in your room. Everybody needs something to say *no* to!"

Sensory handicaps may not be quite so visible as physical impairments but they may be just as challenging both for the senior adult and for caregivers. In mid-life we get a distant early warning of visual changes when we put on bifocals. The aging ear may also lose some of its responsiveness to sounds of higher frequencies.

Older adults who have poor sight or hearing may tend to avoid situations in which they feel inadequate or left out. Much can be done, however, by caregivers, to enhance communication and reduce isolation. Be alert to the indications of impairment in senior adults you visit. If a person wears glasses but doesn't have them on, ask if they would like to have them. If hearing is better in one ear than another, try to speak toward the good side. Speak distinctly, in lower tones, not necessarily louder. Occasionally, what appears to be apathy or confusion is greatly reduced when people can hear or see what is going on.

Of all the impairments of later life, perhaps none is so greatly feared or so baffling to family and friends as is the mental handicap known as dementia. Once regarded as the inevitable consequence of old age, mental confusion among older people is now understood to be the result of disease.

Recent research has established that the cause of most impairment in the mental functioning of older people is a disorder known as Alzheimer's Disease. It is a progressive loss of intellectual capacity for which at present there is no cure. It often first appears as disturbed memory, as when a person becomes disoriented in previously familiar surroundings. Because mental confusion can result from many causes, some of which are reversible, the family of a confused older person should be urged to secure a careful medical evaluation of their loved one.

As Alzheimer's Disease progresses, family caregivers are subject to severe emotional and physical stress. The victim may have a tendency to wander, to be up at all hours of the night, and to require around-the-clock attention. A helpful resource for family members is the guidebook *The 36-Hour Day* by Nancy L. Mace and Peter V. Rabins.[26] Local support groups offer help to family caregivers. For the address of local chapters, write to the Alzheimer's Disease and Related Disorders Association, Inc., 360 N. Michigan Ave., Chicago, IL 60601.

Dementia reduces the person's capacity for abstract thinking. What this means for caregivers is that more attention must be given to the feeling side of communication. It is often still possible for those who take the time and make the effort to create that special kind of closeness which gratifies both the older person and the caregiver.

Two avenues are still open for communicating in spite of confusion. One is verbal and the other nonverbal. The verbal route consists of efforts to talk with the impaired person in an effort to discover the meaning in what may at first seem to be nonsense. This requires us to think in symbolic terms, and to hear more of the feelings being expressed, rather than worry over logical inconsistencies.[27]

For example, when my wife's mother says to us: "I don't know why Mac has been gone so long. I think he was taking a load of furniture to Lenoir," we don't fret over the fact that Mac, her husband, died in 1977. We don't tell her he'll soon be back. We focus on her feeling, which seems likely to be loneliness or grief. "Have you been missing Mac?" we may ask, or we may say, "It has been a long time since you saw him, and you are anxious to see him again."

Family members who watch their loved one's ability to think slowly dwindle away are in effect having to mourn while the person is still alive. They may feel helpless and frustrated to make things better.

A change in perspective has helped some caregivers to feel less defeated. They stop trying to hold back the inevitable. They redefine their relationship to their loved one. Instead of seeing themselves as givers and their loved ones as weak, they put themselves into the role of learners. Instead of working for a certain response, they learn to enjoy the spontaneous response of their loved one to the simple joys of the moment—the beauty of a flower, the smile of a child.

One family member who changed her way of relating made a further reassuring discovery about her cousin: "His character and personality were unaltered by his dissolving ability to think. Although he no longer knew who anyone was, he related to all persons with courteous charm. . . . He knew instantly when he was loved."[28]

Nonverbal forms of communication can be helpful in relating to individuals who have difficulty in understanding verbal messages. A wave of the hand, a smile, a warm handclasp, or a hug can convey friendliness, affection, and closeness when words fail.

Physical touch is the most powerful form of nonverbal communication. Although it should not be overused, or abused, it can often make contact when other means fail. It is usually welcomed if it is appropriate to the degree of closeness felt in the relationship.[29]

Conclusion

At the beginning of this chapter, I mentioned two of my friends who taught me something about what it means to retire. Now at its conclusion, I am aware that they are only two of a much larger number of senior adults who have been my mentors. My experience with some of them is shared here. I take this opportunity to express my gratitude to them.

My experience has confirmed Henri Nouwen's insight that caring with the aging begins by allowing the aging to care for us. "When in careful listening we lift up the story of one person into the larger story of mankind," he noted, "we also connect the human story with God's story."[30]

While we learn from all with whom we minister, only senior adults have the wisdom that comes from length of days. As we share the journey of those who are moving toward the light, our own faith is increased, and we sense anew God's purpose for us for all our days—to glorify Him and to declare His love to the world.

Notes

1. Zechariah 14:7, KJV.

2. Bernice L. Neugarten, "Personality Change in Late Life: A Developmental Perspective," *The Psychology of Adult Development and Aging,* ed. Carl Eisdorfer and M. Powell Lawton (Washington, D.C.: American Psychological Association, 1973).

3. Robert J. Havighurst, *Developmental Tasks and Education,* 3rd ed. (New York: David McKay Co., 1972).

4. Ibid.

5. Evelyn M. Duvall, *Family Development,* 3rd ed. (Philadelphia: J. B. Lippincott, 1967).

6. Erik H. Erikson, *Childhood and Society,* 2nd ed. (New York: W. W. Norton, 1963).

7. _____, ed., *Adulthood* (New York: W. W. Norton, 1978).

8. Ibid.

9. Robert C. Peck, "Psychological Developments in the Second Half of Life," *Middle Age and Aging,* ed. Bernice L. Neugarten (Chicago: University of Chicago Press, 1968).

10. Ecclesiastes 12:3-5a *Good News Bible.*

11. E.g., Ernest Becker, *The Denial of Death* (New York: The Free Press, 1973).

12. Horace Kerr, *How to Minister to Senior Adults in Your Church* (Nashville: Broadman Press, 1980), p. 73.

13. Elaine M. Brody, "Aged Parents and Aging Children," *Aging Parents,* ed. Pauline K. Ragan (Los Angeles: University Press, 1979), also, Ethel Shanas, "The Family As a Social Support System in Old Age," *The Gerontologist,* 19 (1979) 169-74.

14. E.g., Bernice L. Neugarten, professor of human development, University of Chicago. See Michael Briley, "You and Your Aging Parent," *Dynamic Years,* 13 (Sept.-Oct., 1978), p. 19.

15. John H. Westerhoff and William H. Willimon, *Liturgy and Learning Through the Life Cycle* (New York: The Seabury Press, 1980), pp. 149-52.

16. Kerr, p. 61.

17. Erdman Palmore, "Facts on Aging: A Short Quiz," *The Gerontologist,* 17 (1977) 318.
18. Sarah-Patton Boyle, *The Desert Blooms* (Nashville: Abingdon Press, 1983), p. 26.
19. Ibid.
20. Ibid.
21. Palmore, *The Gerontolgist,* 17 (1977) 317.
22. Boyle, p. 49.
23. Robert N. Butler, "The Life Review: An Interpretation of Reminiscence in the Aged," *Psychiatry,* 26 (1963) 65-76.
24. Isaiah 43:16,18-19, *Good News Bible.*
25. Boyle, p. 143.
26. Nancy L. Mace and Peter V. Rabins, *The 36-Hour Day* (Baltimore: The Johns Hopkins University Press, 1981).
27. Albert L. Meiburg, "Pastoral Communication with the Confused," *Pastoral Psychology,* 31 (Summer, 1983) 277.
28. Boyle, p. 190.
29. Meiburg, *Pastoral Psychology,* p. 274.
30. Henri J. J. Nouwen, "Care and the Elderly," *Aging and the Human Spirit,* eds. Carol LeFevre and Perry LeFevre (Chicago: Exploration Press, 1981) 291-96.

Additional Bibliography

Bianchi, Eugene C. *Aging as a Spiritual Journey.* New York: Crossroads, 1982.

Boyle, Sarah-Patton. *The Desert Blooms: A personal adventure in growing old creatively.* Nashville: Abingdon Press, 1983.

Clements, William M., ed. *Ministry with the Aging.* San Francisco: Harper and Row, 1981.

Freeman, Carroll B. *The Senior Adult Years.* Nashville: Broadman, 1979.

Gray, Robert M. and Moberg, David O. *The Church and the Older Person.* Grand Rapids: Eerdmans, 1977.

Hiltner, Seward, ed. *Toward a Theology of Aging.* New York: Human Sciences Press, 1975.

LeFevre, Carol and Perry, eds. *Aging and the Human Spirit: A Reader in Religion and Gerontology.* Chicago: Exploration Press, Chicago Theological Seminary, 1981.

Maves, Paul B. and Cedarleaf, J. Lennart *Older People and the Church.* Nashville: Abingdon, 1949.

Meiburg, Albert L. "Aging Is Becoming—Who We Are." *Search.* 11:2, Winter, 1981, 59-64.

________. "Meeting the Unique Spiritual Needs of the Aging." *Bulletin, American Protestant Hospital Association.* 47:1, Winter, 1983, 26-29; 32.

_____. "Pastoral Communication with the Confused." *Pastoral Psychology*. 31:4 Summer, 1983.

_____. "Understanding Senile 'Confusion': Sources and Stages." *Pastoral Psychology*. 31:3, Spring, 1983, 161-169.

Silverstone, Barbara and Hyman, Helen Kandel. *You and Your Aging Parents*. New York: Pantheon, 1976.

Stagg, Frank. *The Bible Speaks on Aging*. Nashville: Broadman, 1981.

Thorson, James A. and Cook, Thomas C. *Spiritual Well-Being of the Elderly*. Springfield, Ill: Charles C. Thomas, 1977.

7
Toward a Holistic Approach to Caring
James E. Hightower, Jr.

This book divided persons into age groups, and the authors spoke to developmental tasks faced by persons from birth to death.

Pastoral care would be much simpler if it could be that cut and dried. Unfortunately it is not. Adults in the twilight years still deal with the issues of dependence/independence found in the preschool years. Likewise adolescents are in some ways as much on the go as adults in their middle years.

This chapter will examine what it means to care, who is called to care, what skills are needed in caring, and pastoral care in time of crisis that transcends age or developmental task boundaries.

Persons need to be viewed as whole. Certainly we do pass through both chronological age and development task. But that is not the complete story.

What Does It Mean to Care?

Proverbs 20:5 is a beautiful example of the importance of counsel: "Counsel in the heart of man is like deep water; but a man of understanding will draw it out."

The religious counselor is one who is inherently helpful.

Charles Traux and Kevin Mitchell identified three qualities that persons use in helping other persons. They are: accurate empathy; nonpossessive warmth; and genuineness.

Accurate Empathy

Have you ever been with a friend for a brief period of time and known something was wrong? That's accurate empathy—feeling what someone else feels. Knowing that your friend hurts may be picked up in a multitude of ways.

147

- The person's voice may sound flat and depressed.
- The person may have a blank stare on his/her face rather than varied emotions.
- The person who is normally quiet may be agitated and unable to sit still.
- The person who is always on the go may be so still as to appear ill.
- How the person sits, looks at you (or doesn't look at you), or a hundred other ways are used to tell that something is wrong.

Nonpossessive Warmth

My colleague at the Sunday School Board, Fred McGhee, defines this as "being able to respond with affection to the other person's need rather than using the other person to meet one's own need."

Pastoral counselors will be attuned to getting their personal needs met. However, these needs should be met by persons other than the hurt one with whom we are working. The pastoral counselor will build a support system in which his or her needs can be met. Pastors who counsel also need to find someone who can counsel them. It is not fair to a hurting person to bring my hurt into the counseling session.

Nonpossessive warmth is also caring for persons just as they are. Too often religious helpers give the impression that "I will care for you when (or if) you get your life back in order." The call to Christian helpers is to give warmth to persons whether they ever "get their life back in order again."

This idea of nonpossessive warmth is exemplified in Jesus of Nazareth. Jesus was in Jericho when He called a man named Zacchaeus down from a tree. Zacchaeus was the town's derelict. Everyone knew he was no good. People probably related to him in the "when you get your life straight, then we'll like you" mode. Everyone . . . except Jesus.

Jesus said, "Zacchaeus come down, I'm going to your house today." No strings attached; I'll care for you just like you are. In the warmth of fellowship and eating together Zacchaeus was converted. His conversion also led him to right his wrongs of the past.

People had tried the judgmental "if you do what we say, then we'll like you" method with Zacchaeus. Now the master showed the people of Jericho, and us, a new way.

It is the way of nonpossessive warmth.

Genuineness

Helpers will always have trouble here if they have a hard time accepting themselves. This element of caring is best described as sincerity. People who hurt need to know that the one who is helping them is real. Our model for genuineness is Jesus Christ who related to people at all times with openness and honesty. We are called to follow Him as we learn to accept ourselves and to minister to others.

Who Is Called to Care?

The ministry of the church is shared by all who name Jesus as Lord. Baptists and others accept the doctrinal view of the priesthood of all believers. This issue of soul competency was stated as E. Y. Mullins's second axiom of religion.

"The religious axiom: All souls have an equal right to direct access to God."[1]

The corollary to this must also be true. If we have direct access to God, we are called to function as priests before God. A part of the priestly task is to care for persons. Pastoral ministry (caring for folks from birth to death) is more than a function for ordained clergy; it is every Christian's task.

First Peter 2:4-10 speaks clearly to us about our priesthood.

> To whom coming, as unto a living stone, disallowed indeed of men, but chosen of God, and precious, Ye also, as lively stones, are built up a spiritual house, an holy priesthood, to offer up spiritual sacrifices, acceptable to God by Jesus Christ. Wherefore also it is contained in the scripture, Behold, I lay in Sion, a chief corner stone, elect, precious: and he that believeth on him shall not be confounded.
>
> Unto you therefore which believe he is precious: but unto them which be disobedient, the stone which the builders disallowed, the same is made the head of the corner, And a stone of stumbling, and a rock of offence, even to them which stumble at the word, being disobedient: whereunto also they were appointed.
>
> But ye are a chosen generation, a royal priesthood, an holy nation, a peculiar people; that ye should shew forth the praises of him who hath called you out of darkness into his marvellous light: Which in time past were not a people, but are now the people of God: which had not obtained mercy, but now have obtained mercy.

Verse 4 reminds us how we do ministry. As we "come to him" (Jesus

Christ), we are enabled to do ministry. Ministry is done in the name of Jesus Christ; it is also done through Jesus Christ.

Then the epistle writer tells us three aspects of this priesthood.

We are called to be community. In verse 5 the epistle writer gives us a new dimension to our faith in Jesus Christ. The gospel word is that Christians are always found in community. One person said: "The freelance Christian, who would be a Christian but is too superior to belong to the visible church upon earth in one of its forms, is simply a contradiction in terms."

You and I are living stones built into a spiritual house. That is where caring should always come from—the fellowship of believers.

Dietrich Bonhoeffer was one of the great Christians of our time. As a Nazi resister, he formed an underground seminary. For this special community he wrote a discipline that is published under the title *Life Together.* This is what he said about community in those extreme circumstances. "Christianity means community through Jesus Christ. No Christian community is more or less than this. Whether it be a brief, single encounter or the daily fellowship of years, Christian community is only this. We belong to one another only through and in Jesus Christ."[2]

The electronic church is a popular expression of present-day religious life in this country. However, this dimension of the contemporary religious scene cannot provide a sense of community like a local church.

We are called to be priests. The gospel word is that all Christians are priests. In the Old Testament only the priest had direct access to God. Then only the High Priest had access to God on the high holy day of the year. Then through Jesus Christ, the veil that separated the priest from the holy of holies was torn apart. You and I (clergy and laity alike) became priests who could function before God.

But what does a priest do? The Latin word for priest is *pontifex.* It means bridge builder. The priest is one who has access to God and whose task it is to bring others to God. The priest is a bridge builder.

The priest also brought the people's sacrifice to God. Paul gave this a new meaning for this new priest. Romans 12:1 declares, "Present your bodies a living sacrifice, holy, acceptable unto God, which is your reasonable service."

Radical commitment is required. Once an animal brought to the priest would suffice. Now I must bring myself: my work, my family life, my relationships, my worship.

We who are New Testament priests are bridge builders between God and persons and person to person. Isn't that what pastoral care is? We have become God's own caring people. But we are God's people with a purpose. It is our individual privilege and our collective function as the church to care for persons. As we do this we praise God who called us from darkness to light.

Who is called to care? All Christians are ministers. That says to pastors who are called to "equip the saints for the work of the ministry" (Eph. 4:12) that ways need to be developed to train laypeople in ministry. Re-education is called for in this area so that when laypeople make a quality pastoral visit, it is identified as that by the pastor, the visitor, and the one visited.

What Skills Are Needed to Care?

Authentic Person

Remember Traux and Mitchell's three characteristics of a caring person? The third was genuineness. That's what I am talking about. The person who gives care must be perceived as being real. Sidney Jourard expressed it in these terms. "Authentic being means being oneself, honestly, in one's relations with his fellows. It means taking the first step at dropping pretense, defenses, and duplicity."[3]

The first skill we bring to caring for others is ourself. It is more than just bringing myself; it is bringing my real self with my joy, pain, pleasure, and suffering. It is bringing the me that is willing to let other people into my life. It is, as Henri Nouwen said, being a "wounded healer."

Listening Person

In Bonhoeffer's discipline for the underground seminary, he wrote about the ministry of listening: "The first service that one owes to others in the fellowship consists in listening to them. Just as love to God begins with listening to His Word, so the beginning of love for the brethren is learning to listen to them. It is God's love for us that He not only gives us His Word but also lends us His ear. So it is His work that we do for our brother when we learn to listen to him.[4]

My boyhood home was next to the Episcopal rectory. When my home church ordained me, my next door neighbor, the Episcopal rector, gave me two ordination gifts. One was the book entitled *The Awesome Power of the Listening Ear* by John Drakeford. He knew something I didn't know but needed to learn. Nothing in ministry beats listening!

Pastoral care is a congregational task. Laypersons are often ahead of their pastor in the caring skill of listening. Preachers are taught to be tellers, not listeners. Through the pastor's preaching/teaching ministry we are more interested in monologue than dialogue. Bonhoeffer's words need to be the preacher's theme. God, in his love for us, gave us both His Word and His Ears. So how can you be a better listener? Let me enumerate several ideas.

1. *Give your full attention to the one who is speaking.*— Nothing substitutes for listening to a person. Listen to the verbal message, but also listen to the nonverbal message. What part of the story is so hard to describe that the person sounds as if he is chewing cotton? How is this person sitting or is he too nervous to sit for any length of time? What the person chooses not to say is often more important than what is said.

Listen also for voice-related clues. Perhaps part of a story is so hard to tell the person is on the verge of tears. Listen for joy-filled parts of the story that bubble out like a flowing brook. Listen for the flat, emotionless tone that denotes depression.

2. *Listen to the feelings as well as the facts of a person's story.*—Hearing the facts (or the message) is only one half the task of a caregiver. The more important task is to hear a person's feelings. Is he feeling joy, depression, anger, guilt, regret, or some other emotion?

Let's say an adolescent comes to you and says:

"I got so mad at my mother last night; I really told her off. I even told her to get out of my room and never come back."

The facts are a family fight. The feeling being talked about is anger. But my hunch would be that the feeling being expressed is guilt or sorrow.

If the minister doesn't hear the expression of guilt, the teenager could well go away not being helped.

When a person gives care to another person, many feelings can be expressed in a short period of time. A major task of the counselor is to help the person focus on the dominate feelings.

3. *Be aware of how intense the person telling the story is.*—Often the sheer intensity of the storyteller will be a vital clue to the minister.

If a person comes in with a story of horror in family relations and tells it with a smile, the counselor should beware. How do you tell horror stories and smile all the while? Perhaps the person hasn't allowed the awful reality to sink in yet.

Is the dominant feeling being expressed mild, moderate, or strong? Intensity tells you a great deal.

4. *Don't be afraid to formulate a response in your mind before answering.*—Identify the content. Identify the dominant feeling. Then respond.

A response to our hotheaded friend might be:

"Are you feeling guilty over talking so harshly to your mother last night?"

5. *Let your tone be empathetic and genuine.*—Let's stay with our teenage friend a minute. Remember how hard it was to declare your own personhood as a teenager. Recall those years before judging our young friend. That's what empathy is—trying to feel what someone else is feeling.

But also be genuine. As an adult it would be fine to let this teenager know you also understand his mother must be hurt. Don't deny the reality in order to make someone feel better. Yet, in facing reality, do it respectfully, not degrading the person.

6. *Check the accuracy of your responses with the person.*—You may have totally misread the situation. Give the person the right to tell you. Most people will give you several chances to hear their feelings before moving on to someone else.

Ask yourself the question: "Did my responses help this person explore the problem in a more helpful way?" If so, it was a good response.

Now we will look at some barriers to listening.

1. *Don't ask too many questions.*—Allow persons to tell what they want you to know. Seldom does finding out more facts aid you in listening better.

2. *Don't finish people's thoughts for them.*—It is humanly impossible to know precisely what another is going to say.

3. *Don't preach.*—"Shoulds" and "oughts" only leads to barriers in listening to people. Believe that the Holy Spirit is powerful enough to work in each person's life. Allow the Spirit to guide this person.

4. *Don't deny the reality of feelings.*—We've all had it happen. Someone

comes to us feeling dumb. Our response is: "It's not true; you're one of the smartest people I know." That may be true; but if they're feeling dumb, they leave you feeling either misunderstood, rejected, or both.

5. *Don't be afraid of silence.*—Silence can be a friend if we let it. Even if it is a definite silence or a silence of withdrawing, it may be necessary for the person's sake. Silence can be creative.

6. *Don't listen just so you can tell your own story.*—Listening to someone just so I can tell my story is not listening at all.

> I bend a sympathetic ear
> To other people's woes,
> However dull it is to know
> Their real or fancied throes.
> I pay to every gloomy line
> Attention undiminished.
> Because I plan to start on mine
> The moment theirs are finished.[5]

Seneca, the Roman poet, said:

> Listen to me for a day—an hour!—
> a moment! lest I expire in my ter-
> rible wilderness, my lonely silence!
> O God, is there no one to listen?

If you are going to care for folks from birth to death, you will have to dedicate yourself to listening to them.

Preaching Is Caring

Six Characteristics of a Caring Sermon[6]

1. *A sermon has a caring quality when the preacher is perceived as being a real human being.*—A significant part of any sermon is the sermon deliverer. When the preacher is willing to share his humanity, his message will be more sincere. When the pastor must *act* like a plastic saint, his message will not be genuine. The preacher must give evidence that he too is human with all the joys and hurts that entails.

2. *A sermon has a caring quality when it answers questions people are asking.*—The sermon should be grounded in Scripture but originated from human need. The sermon should reveal understanding of human need. When the preacher is a real person speaking to a real need the platform is set for a face-to-face encounter with God!

3. *A sermon has a caring quality when it has given the congregation a chance to participate.*—Persons learn through activity? Begin a Bible study group that helps you gain insight from the Scripture. Start a worship committee that aids in planning, implementing, and evaluating worship. Enlist deacons and other lay leaders to help in the worship event.

Use different age groups. Children and teenagers can lead God's people in worship also. This is a signal to them, "My pastor thinks I'm a real person!" People learn best through activity, not passivity.

4. *A sermon has a caring quality when it appeals to as many of the senses as possible.*—One of the beauties of observing the Lord's Supper is that it can appeal to all five senses. The traditional sermon appeals to one sense (hearing) and in a limited way to sight. Each sense the pastor can add to the sermon makes a stronger caring sermon.

5. *A sermon has a caring quality when it builds on past experience.*—At times the wise pastor will lay extensive groundwork before preaching on a given issue. If a church has been plagued by conflict, the pastor will need to spend much time in relationship building, listening, and interpreting before publicly confronting the issue in a sermon.

Previous situations in an individual's or a communities' life will affect learning. The wise pastor uses this to good advantage for the kingdom's sake.

6. *A sermon has a caring quality when it helps persons meet their needs for security, mastery, and belonging.*—Security will help persons build their self-esteem and affirm their worth in God's sight. Mastery will help persons see their lives in such a way that they are free to choose for or against God. Belonging will affirm the sense of community found in the local church. Belonging needs will also be met as the invitation is extended to join this household of faith.

Caring is not complete until a new awareness of truth has broken through or until behavior has been changed. Preaching that is caring must be directed at enhancing a person's or community's knowledge or changing their behavior in the light of Jesus Christ.

Pastoral Care in Times of Crisis

Some crises of life transcend chronological age and/or developmental task. Gail Sheeby in her book *Pathfinders* refers to these as life accidents. No one plans for these occasions; they happen. Two crisis events will be discussed here—hospitalization and grief.

While skills will be emphasized in this section, the caring minister will always remember the developmental stage that the person is in.

Ministry to persons as individuals always takes into account who the person is and what stage of life they are in. Viewing persons as holistic beings also gives room for a person not to fit any theory of developmental stages.

Ministry to the Hospitalized

The following is a pastoral conversation of mine as a beginning Clinical Pastoral Education student. It is not presented as model ministry but as an example of ministry. C. represents the chaplain/minister, P. represents the hospitalized patient.

The patient's first name was J. R. I was surprised to discover a woman in the room. I noticed the room had several bouquets of flowers and a fruit basket. It did not look like a room a person had occupied that afternoon. I made a mental note to check on how long she had been there.

As I entered, she was picking up the telephone to make a call. Responding to my knock, she said:

P. Come in.

C. Hello, Ms. M?

P. Yes.

C. (*I began with a little chuckle and said*) When I saw the name J. R. I did not expect to find you—I've never heard J. R. as a woman's name before.

P. (*chuckling*) I know—that is not a common name—most people just don't admit it surprises them.

C. Well, let me introduce myself. I am Chaplain Hightower from the hospital. I wanted to visit with you and see what is going on with you.

P. I'm glad you came by. You know I had a hysterectomy last week. I came through it with very little worry and just fine. Later that week they found a lump in my right breast—they X-rayed me and the Doctor said that lump was nothing, but found a mass in my left breast that he said must be seen about. He may even do a radical (*her eyes begin to cloud up at this point*). You know, I do not understand why I could go through the hysterectomy with no problem and I am scared to death of this operation in the morning.

C. How do you see the surgery tomorrow as being different from the surgery last week?

P. I am really afraid they will find something tomorrow that we cannot handle—with the hysterectomy it was routine. I'd just had some trouble and that was the easiest cure. I'm afraid they will find cancer and I'll die. (*At this point, the patient began to sob and in her sobbing looked at me—I reached my hand out to her and before my hand got to hers, she reached and met mine. This seemed to tell her that I understood her need to cry.*)

Then we begin talking about the fear of death and the possible results of the forthcoming surgery. The dialogue seemed to center on the fear of leaving a husband and two children behind instead of the fear of possible radical surgery. After a few minutes of this discussion, the conversation followed this course.

C. Ms. M., I hope you will find some new spiritual resources or be able to call on some old ones to help you face the anxiety before surgery and to face whatever the report may be tomorrow. I want you to know I will be praying for you as you face the events of tomorrow. (*Her look seemed to say let's do it now.*) Sometimes I pray with people in their room. Would you like this, or should I remember you later?

P. Let's pray now, please.

C. Dear Lord, I thank you for my new friend. I trust this friend and all her needs to your care. We acknowledge the fear of death but we also acknowledge our faith in you. Lord, we pray you will bless all involved in the events of tomorrow and especially do we pray you will bless those she loves so much. We are your children and we trust our cares into your hands. Amen.

P. I know I'll face this surgery with new faith. Thank you for coming.

C. God bless you. (*I left*)

The next day I checked with the Chaplain on her floor and asked to go back up and see her.

Upon arriving on the floor, I checked with the Nurse as to the outcome of the surgery. The report was negative so the radical surgery was not done.

The head R.N. overheard me asking, and she got up and came to the desk. She wanted to know if I was the Chaplain who talked with her last evening. I told her I was, and she thanked me for the time I spent with her. She said, "I heard you cried with her last night; now please go down and rejoice with her." I thanked the nurse and went to the patient's room.

C. Hey, I hear you have good news.

P. (Smiling) I was hoping you would come by so I could tell you. Thank you so much for praying to God for me.

C. I'm glad I got to meet you and share some of this experience with you. (*She then introduced me to her husband and Mother. We talked briefly, then I left.*)

Several things strike me that I did correctly.

1. *I knocked before entering the room.* You must remember that a hospital room is both livingroom and bedroom. Depending on the patient's condition, it might be bathroom also. The patient's room is a private place. Don't enter before you knock.

2. *I was honest.* I was surprised to find a young woman named J. R. I was genuine in saying so. The patient's response was: "Most people just don't admit it surprises them." That started us on an honest relationship.

3. *I identified myself.* Even if you are the pastor visiting a faithful member you've known for ten years, identify yourself. It is possible the person is so medicated as to be confused or has seen so many strangers coming in and out of the room, he simply does not recognize you.

Be careful how you identify yourself. Don't use the academic title of *Doctor* in a hospital setting.

I have a friend who was recently awarded his doctorate. He was so proud of it he used the title wherever he went. Soon after receiving the degree, he moved to a new pastorate. One of his first visits was to a female member of the church who was hospitalized. He had not previously met her.

Upon entering the room he said, I'm Dr. S_____.

The lady immediately said "Thank goodness, you're here. This incision is driving me crazy." Her subsequent action was intended for a doctor, not her new pastor.

Needless to say my friend was embarrassed, and his new church member was humiliated.

Identify yourself as a minister, not as "Doctor so and so."

4. *I let the patient express her emotions.* She was visibly upset and she had a right to be. I let her know by a simple touch that it was permissible to cry in my presence.

I also allowed her to use two words that are taboo in our culture— death and cancer. For J. R. naming the monster gave her some control over it.

5. *I let the patient take the lead in discussing her problem.* I made an open-ended comment. "I wanted to visit with you and see what is going on with you." That let her take the lead with the conversation. It put her in the control position.

6. *I helped her call on her own spiritual resources.* This was done by acknowledging her need for prayer.

It should be noted that the follow-up the next day was an important part of the pastoral visit.

Dennis E. Saylor in his book *"—And You Visited Me!"* offers these twelve suggestions for hospital ministry.[7]

1. Knock before entering a patient's room.
2. Walk and talk softly.
3. Shake hands only at the patient's request.
4. Have a pleasant facial expression.
5. Be brief.
6. Visit when well.
7. Remember that the patient's condition is personal.
8. Consider the patient's rights.
9. Keep personal problems to yourself.
10. Maintain eye contact.
11. Always identify yourself.
12. Enter the room only if the call light above the door is not on.

Hospitalization happens to persons of all ages. It is a life accident that transcends chronological age or developmental task. It is more often than not viewed as a crisis time for persons. Therefore, ministers are rightly expected to be expert at hospital ministry.

One word needs to be said about children in the hospital. When a child is hospitalized, the minister should visit the child, not just the parents. The pastor should leave the room with that child knowing she is special.

The minister should never underestimate the value of personal presence. Far more valuable than saying the right words or picking up on the person's cues is being there.

Jesus' words "and you visited me" are not to be taken lightly. Physical presence is a major part of caring for folks from birth until death.

Ministry to the Grieving

From birth to death we are grievers. Life might well be defined as a series of mini-griefs interspersed with major grief. We normally associate grief with someone's death. "Her husband died and she is grieving," we say. Yet this woman has known many mini-griefs before this time. What are some of them that she and other persons face?

Leaving her parent's home to attend college or to marry was a grief experience for both her and her parents. It was the death of one relationship (or at least its reconstruction) and the birth of a new one.

The birth of a child, particularly the first child, breaks the death of one way of life and birth to a new way. Post-partum blues is the acknowledgment of that grief.

The loss of a job can be a major grief to a productive, energetic person.

Buying a home can cause anxiety over the financial responsibility, and it can herald a new era of independence from parents.

Moving from a beloved city to another city or a beloved house to a new residence can be a source of grief.

The failure of significant plans for jobs, security, family, or parents can cause grief.

An illness or hospitalization can cause us to grieve over our mortality and/or our declining physical powers.

You can list occasions of grief in your own life. Any loss causes physical and emotional reactions that we call grief.

I lead several grief workshops each year. They are attended in large part by pastors. I am amazed to find that typically only 3 out of 10 have heard of the book *On Death and Dying*.[8] It is a significant work in which Elisabeth Kubler-Ross traced five discernable stages in the grief process.

1. *Denial and isolation.*—This is the feeling "No, not me, it cannot be true." Denial is used by virtually everyone. I believe it should be seen as a gift from God. It allows us to protect ourselves from tragic news

until we can muster courage to hear it. A feeling of loneliness and isolation is also very prevalent during this stage.

2. *Anger.*—The anger stage asks the question "Why me?" The first stage of denial cannot be maintained any longer so it is replaced by feelings of rage, resentment, and anger. Often this anger is given to family members, employers, doctors, nurses, ministers. It is a way of saying: "I'm not finished yet; you have to listen to me."

3. *Bargaining.*—If anger has not worked to take away our hurt, then perhaps asking politely will. We learn as children that asking nicely gets one further with parents than demanding. In the bargaining stage we ask God politely. "God, if I become a preacher will you get me out of this mess?" or "God, I'll never hit my wife again if you'll make her come back to me." Bargaining is often filled with irrational fears and excessive guilt.

4. *Depression.*—When the person realizes the great loss he/she has sustained, then depression sets in. For the terminally ill person this depression may be a form of preparatory grief where impending loss is prepared for. It is a tool used to prepare more easily. Whether grief is a situational loss or a preparation to die, the person should be allowed to be depressed—to mourn the loss.

5. *Acceptance.*—This is not a happy state; rather it is almost devoid of feeling. It is a signal that the struggle is over. It is the woman who can say: "I lost a breast to cancer." It is the man who can say: "After 34 years with the company, I lost my job."

Kubler-Ross did not say we go through these stages sequentially so that stage 1 leads to stage 2, and so forth. Rather, a person can be in acceptance today (or this hour) and in denial the next day (or next hour). Grief is a journey with crooked roads and many turn-back signs; it is not an interstate highway connecting two points at the shortest distance.

Persons grieve regardless of chronological age or developmental task. The preschool child who loses a pet grieves. The middle age child who moves from one town to another grieves. The adolescent who loses a first "love" to another girl or boy grieves. The young adult who doesn't get the job hoped for grieves. The adult whose last child leaves home grieves. The older adult grieves failing health or loss of sight and/or hearing.

From birth to death we are grievers. What can ministers do to care for persons who grieve?

1. *Ministers can be physically present.*—In grief-education workshops, my most often asked question is: "What do you say to someone who is grieving?" I do not believe a grieving person will remember what you say, unless it is so unfeeling as to offend them. What grieving people will remember is whether or not you were present with them.

2. *Ministers can listen.*—Many pastors feel they are called to tell not to listen. God's love is proven to us in that He gave us His Word to speak and His ear to listen. Listen to a person in both content and feelings. Often our own fear of grief will not permit us simply to sit with one who is grieving.

3. *Ministers can help mobilize a support system for the griever.*—The church can express itself as an extension of God's love when people will risk caring.

4. *Ministers can be genuine.*—If you are uncomfortable in the face of grief, acknowledge that feeling. Then find someone to help you work on it. The more comfortable you are in the face of grief, the more you will be able to minister to the grieving.

Conclusion

Pastoral ministry is caring for people. Our preaching, our leading, and our caring should be centered around the task of caring for folks from birth to death in the name of Jesus Christ.

Notes

1. E. Y. Mullins, *The Axioms of Religion* (Philadelphia: American Baptist Publication Society, 1908), p. 53.

2. Dietrich Bonhoeffer, *Life Together,* trans. John W. Doberstein (New York: Harper and Brothers, 1954), p. 21.

3. Sidney M. Jourard, *The Transparent Self* (New York: D. Van Nostrand Company, 1971), pp. 133-34.

4. Bonhoeffer, p. 97.

5. Norman Jaffray, "Good Listener," *Saturday Evening Post,* December 6, 1958, p. 40. Quoted in John Drakeford, *The Awesome Power of the Listening Ear* (Waco: Word Books, 1967), p. 47.

6. This section was adapted from a chapter I prepared for a forthcoming

book compiled by Will Beal, *I'm My Own M.E.!* (Nashville: Convention Press, 1985).

7. Dennis E. Saylor, —*And You Visited Me* (Seattle: Morse Press, Inc., 1979), pp. 45-48.

8. Elizabeth Kubler-Ross, *On Death and Dying* (New York: The Macmillan Co., 1969).

Additional Bibliography

Bailey, Robert W. *Ministering to the Grieving.* Grand Rapids: Zondervan, 1976.

Bryson, Harold T. and Taylor, James C. *Building Sermons to Meet People's Needs.* Nashville: Broadman Press, 1980.

Charry, Dana. *Mental Health Skills for Clergy.* Valley Forge, Pa.: Judson Press, 1971.

Levison, Daniel J. *The Seasons of a Man's Life.* New York: Ballantine Books, 1978.

Sheehy, Gail. *Passages.* New York: E. P. Dutton, 1974, 1976.

_____. *The Pathfinders.* New York: Bantom Books, Inc., 1982.

Sherrill, Lewis Joseph. *The Struggle of the Soul.* New York: The Macmillan Company, 1951.

Stratman, Gary D. *Pastoral Preaching.* Nashville: Abingdon Press, 1973.

Information about Charles Traux and Kevin Mitchell is from a Broadman audiocassette tape by Wayne E. Oates, *A Guide to Counseling.*